THE INFORMATION SYSTEMS
SECURITY OFFICER'S GUIDE

THE INFORMATION SYSTEMS SECURITY OFFICER'S GUIDE

Establishing and Managing an Information
Protection Program

Dr. Gerald L. Kovacich, CFE, CPP, CISSP

BUTTERWORTH–HEINEMANN
Boston • Oxford • Johannesburg
Melbourne • New Delhi • Singapore

Butterworth–Heinemann supports the efforts of American Forests and the Global ReLeaf program in its campaign for the betterment of trees, forests, and our environment.

The Information Systems Security Officer's Guide, by Gerald L. Kovacich.

ISBN 0-7506-9896-9

The publisher offers special discounts on bulk orders of this book.
For information, please contact:
Manager of Special Sales
Butterworth–Heinemann
225 Wildwood Avenue
Woburn, MA 01801-2041
Tel: 781-904-2500
Fax: 781-904-2620

For information on all Butterworth–Heinemann books available, contact our World Wide Web home page at: http://www.bh.com

10 9 8 7 6

Printed in the United States of America

To my father, who is always with me: William M. Kovacich, Chief of Police (Ret.), Whiting, Indiana.

To my mother, who doesn't always understand but always gives love.

To my wife and son, who are always there when I need them the most.

To Motomo Akashi, my mentor, "great sage" and, above all else, friend.

They've all inspired me to achieve my dreams.

"When we enter society at birth, we receive an inheritance from the people who lived before us. It is our responsibility to augment that inheritance for those who succeed us. I feel that all of us owe the world more than we received when we were born."
An Wang
1920–1990

"What do we live for if not to make life less difficult for each other?"
George Eliot

Contents

Foreword

The coming of age of the computer and telecommunication high-tech systems has added a new dimension to security management, called *information systems security* (InfoSec) also referred to as *computer and telecommunications security*. No system seems to be immune from the exploits of hackers, phreakers, and crackers, which have been widely publicized; and industrial and business fraud has increased with the advent of Internet. The traditional methods for managing the investigation of high-tech crimes and frauds have become obsolete, hence the need for InfoSec.

InfoSec requires a new breed of security and law enforcement professionals, who by education, training, and experience have acquired a sufficient understanding of high-tech crime and unauthorized intrusion into the systems to be able to effectively perform and manage investigations. The need and demand for qualified people have prompted a few universities and colleges to begin offering courses at both the undergraduate and graduate levels that supplement the few training programs available. A body of literature is beginning to emerge.

This book is timely because it presents the InfoSec topic with a simple no nonsense way information systems security officers and organization managers of business, industry, and law enforcement agencies may address them. He not only covers the basic technical knowledge necessary for dealing with the problems but provides a systematic approach to becoming and performing as an information systems security officer, both as an InfoSec journeyman and a systems manager.

The Information Systems Security Officer's Guide provides simple guidelines for the academic education, training, and experience necessary for becoming an officer; techniques for obtaining a position; and sets forth the duties and responsibilities of that position. Because an increasing number of both public and private agencies will require information systems security, Dr. Kovacich has included an administrative organization approach to be followed, including planning, implementation, and continuous performance evaluation. He posits the future into the 21st century.

John P. Kenney, Ph.D.
Professor Emeritus

Preface

Over the years, many books have been written about information systems security (InfoSec). These books tend to concentrate on the technical aspects of InfoSec. They discuss what must be done to protect information systems and some even discuss the how-tos. However, I have found that the book I needed when I started in the profession, the type that would really have helped me, was a basic, non-technical book that would guide me through the process of becoming an information systems security officer (ISSO); to understand the basic principles of InfoSec in a business environment; and to establish a practical, business-oriented InfoSec program and organization.

I wanted to know how I could prepare myself for an ISSO position. What education and experience did I need? Then, once I was fortunate to be hired as an ISSO, I wanted to know what I should do first. How do I determine my goals? How do I establish an InfoSec organization? What kind of people should I hire? How do I manage the organization? How do I measure my progress, success, and failures?

These are just some of the questions I would have liked to have found in a book when I looked forward to a career as an ISSO. So, after several decades of learning it "the hard way," through the sometimes arduous process of doing it and learning from success and failure, I decided to start sharing my lessons learned with others.

For several years, I tried to share the information I had learned with those who were just getting started and, also, those who had been ISSOs for some time but still were looking for solutions to some of their information systems security problems.

My InfoSec lectures, given as part of InfoSec-related courses I taught at universities and international conferences, have been attended by various types of professionals. At each of these lectures, the participants asked if I had written a book or had some document that they could take back with them and use as a guide in their company or government agency. Unfortunately, all I could do was to provide them a copy of my briefing slides. So, I saw a need for a book such as this to help guide others through their "unknown InfoSec world."

I also noted that colleges and universities are beginning to include InfoSec-related courses as part of their curriculum. Some schools have even gone so far as to offer undergraduate or graduate courses on the topic of InfoSec. What I found lacking was a basic, introduction to the topic of InfoSec that could be used as a textbook as part of a nontechnical, introductory InfoSec course.

Based on such experiences, this book is written for all those potential ISSOs and those ISSOs who may find some use for ideas put forth in it. This book is written, for the most part, in nontechnical, "noncomputerese." This was done to provide a basic, general overview and understanding of the ISSO position, InfoSec, and how to establish and manage such a program by using a systems approach; that is, from defining the ISSO's working environment to getting an ISSO position through the development and management of an InfoSec program.

This primer on the general field of InfoSec is not a book on how to install a particular type of firewall, access control system, or the like. The first thing that the neo-InfoSec professional must learn is why a firewall and an access control software package are needed. How to use them comes later.

Any discussion of InfoSec should follow a systems approach and, for the most part, that process was used in structuring this book. However, an additional goal was to write each chapter as a stand-alone, major subsystem. Thus, the reader interested in metrics management techniques, for example, could go directly to that chapter to determine the hows and whats of metrics management vis-à-vis InfoSec. So, some redundancy comes with that approach. However, it is believed that the redundancy will also help reinforce some basic ideas.

If read in the order presented, the reader should be able to proceed through an understanding of the world in which the ISSO must work, and how to prepare for and become an ISSO. This is followed by a progressive process of establishing and managing an InfoSec program, and concluding with a look into the world of the 21st century ISSO.

Chapter 1, "Understanding the Information World Environment," describes the current business environment and discusses a short history of technology and its impact on business.

Chapter 2, "Understanding the Business and Management Environment," discusses the philosophy of InfoSec within the business environment, including how to communicate with management so that it clearly understands the issues.

Chapter 3, "The Corporation Incorporated," describes a mythical corporation, The Corporation Incorporated (TCI), in which the ISSO will work. This will assist in providing a practical baseline approach on which the ISSO can build an InfoSec program; in other words, a real-life approach using real scenarios based on many years of experience in the InfoSec profession and as an ISSO.

Chapter 4, "ISSO Career Development," discusses the required education, training, and experience needed to qualify for a position as an ISSO.

Chapter 5, "How to Market Yourself as an ISSO," describes how to "interview by portfolio" to gain the ISSO position you have been looking for.

Chapter 6, "The ISSO's Position, Duties, and Responsibilities," describes and discusses the ISSO position, duties, and responsibilities.

Chapter 7, "The InfoSec Strategic, Tactical, and Annual Plans," discusses the strategic, tactical, and annual InfoSec plans to be used to set the goals and objectives of the InfoSec program and InfoSec organization. These plans sometimes are referred to as *long-range plans, short-range plans, and annual plans.*

Chapter 8, "Establishing an InfoSec Program and Organization," describes how to establish an InfoSec program and organization.

Chapter 9, "Determining and Establishing InfoSec Functions," describes how to determine what InfoSec functions are needed to successfully establish an InfoSec program and how to incorporate those functions into the InfoSec organization's day-to-day work.

Chapter 10, "Metrics Management," discusses the use of metrics management techniques to determine how well the organization is performing its job, to analyze and justify InfoSec costs, to evaluate the impact of downsizing, for briefing management, and so forth.

Chapter 11, "Annual Reevaluation and Future Plans," describes a process that can be used to determine yearly the InfoSec organization's successes and failures and a methodology that can be used to correct the failures and plan for the upcoming years.

Chapter 12, "21st Century Challenges for the ISSO," looks into the future and discusses the challenges and risks to InfoSec in the 21st century.

As a note on the use of the term *InfoSec*, for the purposes of this book, the terms *information systems security, information systems protection, information security, information protection, technology security, computer security, telecommunications security,* and *technology protection* are all incorporated in the term *InfoSec.*

Such terms have different meanings to some and it is not my wish to debate those terms or confuse the reader. The terms all are meant to describe and discuss the security and protection of the computers and telecommunication systems and the information that they store, process, and transmit. The term *InfoSec* will be used as the common one to represent all these terms.

Although this book discusses the ISSO position and InfoSec in a business environment, the information in it can be used by the ISSO employed by a business or government agency. The information presented also is equally applicable to the ISSOs of foreign businesses or government agencies. This is because InfoSec, in any language, in any culture, in any country, is still relative to the protection of information systems and the information that they store, process, and transmit. The same basic principles and methodologies apply.

The need for highly skilled, professional ISSOs undoubtedly will increase in the future. This book is designed to assist the ISSO in successfully meeting the challenges of that position as the business or government agency leader in ensuring that the information and their associated systems are adequately protected at the lowest cost and least impact on the corporation or government agency's costs and schedules.

I hope that the *Information Systems Security Officer's Guide* helps the reader become an ISSO or a better ISSO.

Acknowledgments

Taking on a project such as this takes more than just the author. It takes friends, professional associates, and peers who unselfishly give of their time and effort to help make this book worth publishing.

I am very grateful to all and to a special group that has helped me over the years and again with this project, including Motomo Akashi, industrial security expert (retired); Jerry Ervin, independent security consultant; Bill Boni, director, Coopers Lybrand; and Wira P. Raymond, MBA, president director, PT Citamulia Prajakonsulindo, an Indonesian-based banking and business consulting firm.

I also acknowledge the staff of Butterworth–Heinemann, especially Laurel A. DeWolf, for their time, effort, and support in making this book a reality. Without their support and guidance this book truly could not have been written.

1

Understanding the Information World Environment

CHAPTER OBJECTIVE

The objective of this chapter is to provide the reader with a basic understanding of the changing environment in which the information systems security officer (ISSO) will live and work.

If an ISSO is to be successful, that environment and its technology must be clearly understood. It is the driving force that will dictate what must be done to protect information systems and the information they store, process, and transmit. That environment also will determine how successful the ISSO's information systems security (InfoSec) program will be in providing protection at least cost to the business or government agency.

THE CHANGING WORLD

The importance of InfoSec continues to grow as we become more and more dependent on computers, telecommunication systems, and information systems.

The networking of systems around the world is continuing to expand the global information infrastructure. The importance of InfoSec takes on added meaning because of the increased threats to the systems and the information they store, process, and transmit due to this expanded connectivity.

One cannot address the issue of InfoSec without first addressing the changes brought on by technology and its impact on businesses, government agencies, societies, global economic competition, and the world in general. This changing world has, and will continue to have, a major impact on the ISSO and any InfoSec program.

In the United States and many countries throughout the world, when talking about society, technology, the future, and future trends, one cannot help but bring up the nonfiction writing of three renowned authors: Alvin Toffler, Heidi Toffler, and John Naisbitt.

The Tofflers' writings provide some of the most outstanding looks, not only projecting future trends but also explaining why they are occurring. Their books—*Future Shock, The Third Wave, Powershift, War and Anti-War,* and *Creating a New Civilization,* among others—address the questions of why so many changes are occurring so rapidly and what those trends may mean to our future.

Naisbitt's books—*Megatrends, Megatrends 2000* (coauthored with Patricia Aberdene), and *Megatrends Asia*—provide further looks at our world environment and the trends that are transforming our lives.

In addition, and more important to the ISSO, their information provides a basis for understanding today's global environment and the trends that affect InfoSec, now and in the future.

Understanding this will provide the baseline on which the ISSO can develop and manage an InfoSec program and organization. This is because an InfoSec program and organization must be as dynamic as the environment in which it must operate. Not only is this environment constantly changing, the changes seem to be occurring more and more rapidly, giving the impression of compressing time itself.

The ISSO who does not look ahead at the trends in society, technology, business, global competition, criminal justice systems, crime, and any associated rapid changes will have a stagnant InfoSec program that fails to meet the needs of the business or government agency. An ISSO who cannot meet the needs of the employing business or government agency will need an updated resume, fast!

One just has to look at the United States, which is an advancing information society, to see what is happening to society and the criminal justice system, for example. Is there a relationship between what is happening in the technology arena and its accompanying rapid social and business changes and the need for more security? There at least appears to be a relationship between them.

Before discussing the impacts of technology and the criminal justice system, let's look at society now and in the future, as it seems to be heading. The Tofflers speak of the societies of the world going through or about to go through three "waves."

The First Wave is the agricultural revolution, which has taken thousands of years to develop, mature, and in some countries begin to fade.

According to the Tofflers, this period, at least in the United States, started with the beginning of the human race up to about 1745. Obviously, agriculture is necessary for humans to survive; however, in modern societies, it lacks the force that it once had. During this period, people lived in small and sometimes migratory groups, feeding themselves through fishing, foraging, hunting, and herding. Subsequently, people migrated into clusters, then towns, then cities.

During this First Wave period, information was passed by word of mouth or in written correspondence, usually sent by a courier. People were more dispersed and transportation more primitive. This meant that there was less communication among people. During this period, the number of people who could read or write was relatively few in comparison to the total world population. Therefore, protecting information, although very "human intensive," was not the major consideration it is today.

The threats, such as theft of information in the written form, were minimal, because most of the people of the world could not read or their reading was very limited—although they could destroy the written message. Perhaps, this type of destruction was the first instance of "denial of service"! Information verbally relayed could be misinterpreted or changed, a method that still poses a threat to InfoSec today.

InfoSec during this period was less difficult. In those days, a king who did not want people to talk about the information cut out their tongues. As people became more educated, learning to read and write, the InfoSec challenges increased.

The Second Wave, what the Tofflers' (1994) call the "rise of industrialized civilization," took less than 300 years. This was the age of steel mills, oil refineries, textile plants, mass assembly lines, and the like. The people came together to work in these industries. This period lasted until just a few years after World War II. In the United States, its decline, according to the Tofflers, is believed to have started about 1955 when, for the first time, white-collar workers outnumbered blue-collar workers.

The Second Wave period saw the building of the great cities of the world, the period of great inventions like the telegraph, telephone, air transportation, and computers. This period saw increases in education, mass transportation, and exponential growth in communications—the sharing of information.

The sharing of information became easier due to the invention of communications systems and the increased consolidation of people into large cities. This also made it easier to educate the people, a needed skill to work in the more modern factories and offices of the period.

Sharing information through various communication channels brought new challenges to information protection. The main InfoSec protection methodology that came into its own during this period was cryptography. Cryptography primarily was a government-used InfoSec tool, for the most part because the federal government owned most of the computers.

Although businesses were beginning to look at the use of computers, most were cost-prohibitive and these systems were operated primarily in a stand-alone mode. In other words, the computers did not talk to other computers.

For much of this period, InfoSec for businesses and government agencies consisted of some minimal physical security. As the computer became more sophisticated, the main protection mechanism used for computers changed very little. After all, why worry about such things as access control other than physical security? Not many people knew how to use the computers in the first place. In the beginning of this period, very few people worked in the computer field, and those who did had to know how to "program" with punch cards. Therefore, at first, the threats to information systems and their information were small.

The Third Wave, the age of technology, information, and knowledge, is sweeping across the earth and will have done so in decades not centuries. This Third Wave period, which we are now in, has seen more advances than the First and Second Wave periods combined. This period has seen the rapid growth of technology that is playing a major role in our changing world.

Today, because of the microprocessor, its availability, power, and low cost, the world is building the global information infrastructure (GII). GII is the massive international connection of world computers that will carry business and personal communication as well as that of the social and government sectors of nations. Some say it could connect entire cultures, erase international borders, support "cyber-economies," establish new markets, and change our entire concept of international relations.

GII is based on Internet; and much of the growth of Internet is in developing nations such as Argentina, Iran, Peru, Egypt, Philippines, Russia, Malaysia, and Indonesia. The GII is not a formal project but the result of thousands of individuals', corporations', and governments' need to communicate and conduct business by the most efficient and effective means possible.

One example is the aggressive information infrastructure vision and plans of Malaysia. Malaysia not only wants to aggressively pursue the total integration of information systems in government, businesses, and schools throughout the country, it also wants to establish a "paperless" government! Imagine the InfoSec problems associated with such endeavors. And, of course, it wants to provide global access, such as the Internet, to its citizens while still maintaining its basic culture and religious values. Quite a challenge for the 21st century!

Because of Malaysia's religious beliefs, the Internet access to material considered pornographic is not acceptable. One of that society's struggles will involve how to provide access to the world's information without causing some moral decay of that society. This will be a struggle for many countries; and ISSOs and their InfoSec programs are likely to have a major impact on the society of such developing countries.

Remember the old business saying, "Time is money"? Well, in our world of global competition, that saying is truer now than ever before. An ISSO must understand this better than ever before. InfoSec cannot be a roadblock to business; therefore, one of the challenges to an ISSO is to provide adequate InfoSec in less time.

Another area for the ISSO to consider is that the people in other countries are becoming more educated and gaining a better understanding of the world and technology. There are more world travelers. People in the information age seem to demand more from their government and society while demanding less of themselves. They expect governments, businesses, law enforcement and security officers, and society in general to help them. They expect and demand professionalism at all times. This, too, will have a major impact on the InfoSec programs. More computer-literate people in the world means more access through worldwide networks, as well as more potential threats to the ISSO's company or government agency.

The protection of information systems and the information they process, store, and transmit is of vital concern in this information world. We in the United States already are in the Information Age, and many other nations of the world will soon be there, with more nations to follow them.

Many people look at the use of technology as an excellent tool that can be used now and into the new millennium. It is ushering in a new beginning, the beginning of an age when, with the help of technology, we can make life better for all of us. However, our journey of leaving the old century and starting into the new one will not be without hardship and, yes, maybe even some chaos. This, too, will have an impact on how the ISSO does business.

In many countries, the "Three Waves" are having a simultaneous impact on society, although with various degrees of speed and force. With it comes various degrees of social unrest, conflict, and tensions as the "old wave" supporters try to hold on to the past. Governments, businesses, and people are all being affected, as the Tofflers have pointed out.

In *Creating a New Civilization*, the Tofflers say that the political tensions of today are caused by the conflicts of the industrial age supporters with those of the information age. They believe this is the "super struggle" for the future, due to vested interests.

The ISSO must understand these conflicts and their impact on the business or government agency environment, to be successful in protecting the information systems and the information they store, process, and transmit.

It is important to think about this and reflect on its meaning for the ISSO and the InfoSec responsibilities into the 21st century. As society changes, so must many of the old processes, which include how the InfoSec functions are performed.

ISSOs seem to be reluctant to change, but they must lead the changes in how information systems are securely configured and used. This is the only way to provide the most innovative, flexible, and thus cost-effective InfoSec.

THE CHANGING BUSINESS AND GOVERNMENT ENVIRONMENTS

Many of the changes in the world environment are the basis for the rapid changes in how we do business, both nationally and internationally. Businesses can, and do, adapt to these changes quite rapidly. However, in government agencies, these changes come more slowly and sometimes threaten the very existence of some agencies. For example, the need for a Department of Education and a Department of Commerce seems to be debated with the advent of each congressional session.

One clear example of these changes is the U.S. Post Office (USPO). The USPO must compete with such businesses as Federal Express, DHL, and UPS for the delivery of letters, documents, and packages. However, as more and more people around the world get "on-line" and send electronic mail, legally binding contracts, and other documents through GII and the Internet, the need for an industrial age government agency such as the USPO may become less and less important as information systems provide immediate international communications.

To combat this trend, it appears that the USPO is trying to position itself to be the authenticator of e-mail messages. In others words, stay in business by being the intermediary between the e-mail of senders and receivers to verify and validate that the senders in fact are who they are reported to be.

Now, why is this important to the ISSO? (1) The ISSO will have to be involved in the security issues if the ISSO's business or government agency decides to rely on the USPO for such a service; (2) this also would open up entirely new issues related to privacy concerns, such as would the USPO be able to more easily, and without leaving a trace, read your business's proprietary mail?

In the private sector, telecommunications businesses have become Internet providers. As we look into the future, we see more and more people using the long distance, voice telephone capabilities of Internet, at very little additional cost. One can see that one day the need for a separate telephone instrument in the home or office, as we now know it, may be a thing of the past.

This would be important to the ISSO, because many of the verbal conversations that would take place through the Internet would be sensitive, proprietary business or government information. As the ISSO, you have certain responsibilities that require you to ensure that these conversations can take place securely.

Anyone currently an ISSO and dealing with the problems of Internet's InfoSec knows that compounding the InfoSec problem with the use of verbal communications protection on the Internet would make one want to retire early. At the same time, it offers the ISSO new, unique challenges and, to a certain extent, maybe a little more job security.

One does not have to look far to also see the vital need for an InfoSec program in corporations and government agencies charged with protecting the privacy of individuals whose information is stored, processed, and transmitted by these systems.

THE CHANGING TECHNOLOGY

When we talk about technologies, what do we mean? *Technology* basically is defined as computers and telecommunications systems. In fact, most of today's telecommunications systems are computers. Therefore, the world's telecommunications, technology, systems, and computers sometimes refer to the same things.

Today's computer system environments are based on the microprocessor. The microprocessors have become cheaper and more powerful, the primary cause for their proliferation throughout the world. One systems specialist has found that one megabyte of storage cost $350 in 1975, $30 in 1985, and $1 in 1995! If this rate continues, storage will be almost free in the next century. And, as we all know, the storage of information is the key element needing protection within the company or government agency.

When we think of computers, we sometimes look at them as very complicated devices, when in fact they are not that difficult to understand. Computers are composed of the hardware, the physical pieces; the software, the instructions to the computer that can be altered; and the firmware, instructions embedded on a microprocessor. Together, they are used to process, store, and transmit information.

The more an ISSO knows about how hardware, firmware, and software work, the better the position the ISSO will be in to protect those systems and the information they process, store, and transmit.

Computers have been around for some time. We continue to "celebrate" the "birthday" of the ENIAC, the world's first major computer system. However, the microcomputer, which is much more powerful than the ENIAC, has not been around that long.

In the United States, we have been able to network thousands of systems because of the rapid advances in technology and cheap hardware. We have built the information systems of the United States businesses and government agencies into a major information infrastructure known as the *national information infrastructure* (NII). Stand-alone computer systems (one with no external connections between it and other computers) in the United States today make up a small minority of systems. We cannot function in today's business world and in our government agencies without being connected to other information systems, both nationally and internationally.

The protection of information systems and the information they process, store, and transmit is of vital concern in this information world. We in the United States already are in the information age, with many other nations entering that age, and many more close behind. This will complicate the InfoSec problems of the ISSO.

The ISSO must remember that the InfoSec program must be *service* and *support* oriented. This is of vital importance. The ISSO must understand that the InfoSec program, once it is too costly, outdated, and does not meet the service and support needs of the business or government agency, will be discarded or ignored. So, one of the ISSO's challenges is to network systems nationally and internationally while at the same time protecting company information and systems.

To provide a cost-effective InfoSec program, the ISSO must continually keep up with technology, be familiar with technological changes in general and be intimately familiar with the technology being planned for installation within their business or government agency. The ISSO must understand how to apply InfoSec and integrate InfoSec into, around, and onto the new technology. Failure to do so could leave the system vulnerable to attack. In that case, the ISSO would have a serious problem—possibly a job security problem—if a successful attack occurred due to the newfound vulnerability brought on by the newly implemented technology.

The ISSO could delay installation of the new technology until a suitable InfoSec "umbrella" could be installed. However, in most businesses, this would be a career-limiting or career-ending move. As was previously stated, in today's business world, the phrase "Time is money" is more true than ever. In today's and tomorrow's technologically based environment, *innovation* and *flexibility* are key words for the ISSO to understand and apply to the company's or government agency's InfoSec program.

Therefore, the ISSO has very little choice but to support the installation of the new technology and incorporate InfoSec as effectively and efficiently as possible. And one of the ways to successfully provide that service and support is to keep up with technological changes.

CHANGING CRIMINAL JUSTICE SYSTEMS

Will the importance of InfoSec increase, decrease, or stay about the same as technology and the world changes? Thus far, it appears that InfoSec will increase in importance. If so, the United States criminal justice system and processes undoubtedly also will be affected. The question is, Will it change for the better or worse? If the United States is any indication, it will worsen. Why is this so in such a technologically advanced country? Ironically, technology brings with it rapid social change. The current U.S. criminal justice system was formed during the First and Second Waves. As you recall from the earlier discussions of the Tofflers, these conflicts appear to be inevitable.

One may wonder what impact the criminal justice system has on the ISSO and InfoSec? The answer is simple. The people that steal business' or nations' secrets; damage, destroy, or modify information and systems; and commit other criminal acts are the main reasons why the ISSO and InfoSec program exists. After all, if no one violated laws or company policies and everyone protected information and systems, why would businesses or government agencies need an ISSO or an InfoSec program?

At some point in your career, you will become involved in a high-technology crime investigation and thus will become actively involved in the criminal justice system. You must understand how that system operates or you not only will be at a disadvantage but probably disappointed as well.

As society embraces the Third Wave, it does not wait for the processes of the two prior "waves'" to catch up. One can see the trend of a disintegrating United States criminal justice system, where crime increases faster than the criminal justice system can deal with it. More discretionary arrests and plea-bargaining prosecutions, overburdened court systems, and release of convicted criminals from jails and prisons are indications of this change to a Third Wave society. We seem to be trying to use Second Wave criminal justice system processes and functions to handle Third Wave problems, and it does not seem to be working.

One of the disadvantages of being in a leading technology-based country such as the United States is that one lacks the opportunity to learn from the mistakes of others more advanced. This is an extremely important point, especially when discussing the criminal justice system, because it is the primary system responsible for the prevention of crime and the promotion of social stability of a nation.

If a nation is to be strong enough economically to compete in the world, it must have stability in which businesses can operate and people can have a secure and peaceful life. Lack of security and peace leads to increases in crime. Therefore, it would follow that high-technology crimes likely would increase. In addition, without a good criminal justice system, fraud and other crimes not only will be higher but sap the economic strength from the people, businesses, and the country.

We know that technology is increasing at a rapid rate. Computer-based technology has become a necessary and integral part of businesses, government agencies, and our personal lives. No longer can we efficiently function without the use of today's modern, computer-based technology.

As with any tool, computers, to include telecommunication systems, also can be a target or used as a tool by criminals, also known as techno-criminals. The threats to society, businesses, and government agencies by *techno-criminals* are increasing as our technology and our dependence on technology increases. A 1997 survey conducted by the Computer Security Institute disclosed that computer crimes were increasing and reported losses totaled over $100 million. (For additional information, contact http://www.gocsi.com.)

The techno-criminals, vis-à-vis the world's criminal justice systems, are faced with a system that provides them some measure of immunity in their techno-crimes. For example, the attacks against the U.S. computer systems are becoming more internationally oriented. Today's techno-criminal can attack any place in the world from any place in the world.

What is worse, because of our complicated communication systems, it is difficult to trace the attacks back to the attackers. Also, many countries' laws do not even address the issue of techno-crimes, making it almost impossible to prosecute anyone attacking a U.S. computer from outside the United States. And, because of the political ramifications alone, extradition of these attackers to the United States, or any other country, for prosecution is a complicated and generally impossible task. After all, what nation wants to give up sovereignty over its citizens?

For the ISSO, it is imperative to understand the criminal justice systems of the United States and other countries where the company or government agency does business. The problems with the criminal justice systems, conflicts, and changes will continue to be an underlying force having an impact on the InfoSec functions into the 21st century.

The changes in society, where white-collar crime, fraud, is being perpetrated more and more through the use of computers and telecommunications systems, seems to be an obvious result of the rapid changes in society and our reliance on information systems.

This is understandable, as alluded to earlier, because what once was done by paper and pencil has been automated, like accounting systems. Therefore, although today's criminals have the same motives as in the past, they must now operate in a new environment, a technological environment. If the criminals want to steal money, they must use and attack information systems. To quote an old-time bank robber, "Because that's where the money is."

Because it appears that more crimes are being committed using the computer as a tool to attack other computers and that the trend is likely to continue, the ISSO's responsibilities include an InfoSec program that will assist in minimizing the opportunities for fraud and other crimes through these systems. If such crimes do occur, the ISSO will be expected to play a vital role in the investigation and any disciplinary action or prosecution of the offenders, offering another challenge and opportunity to the ISSO profession.

SUMMARY

1. Technology is changing rapidly and will continue to do so in the future.
2. Changes in technology are changing the way countries, societies, and people in general communicate, interact, and how they view themselves and others.
3. The three periods of change, according to the Tofflers, are the agricultural, industrial, and information periods.
4. Understanding the periods of change, the reasons for the changes, and their impact on the world environment will assist in planning and maintaining a dynamic, effective, and efficient InfoSec program.
5. The ISSO must understand technology and its impact on society, the criminal justice system, and his or her company or government agency to professionally establish and manage an InfoSec program.

REFERENCES

Aburdene, Patricia, and John Naisbitt. *Megatrends 2000*. New York: Avon Books, 1990.

Naisbitt, John. *Megatrends*. New York: Warner Books, 1982.

Naisbitt, John. *Megatrends Asia*. New York: Simon and Schuster, 1996.

Toffler, Alvin. *Future Shock*. New York: Bantam Books, 1971.

Toffler, Alvin. *The Third Wave*. New York: Bantam Books, 1980.

Toffler, Alvin. *Powershift*. New York: Bantam Books, 1990.

Toffler, Alvin, and Heidi Toffler. *War and Anti-War*. Boston: Little, Brown and Company, 1993.

Toffler, Alvin, and Heidi Toffler. *Creating a New World Civilization*. Atlanta: Turner Publishing, 1994.

2

Understanding the Business and Management Environment

CHAPTER OBJECTIVE

The objective of this chapter is to provide the reader with a basic understanding of the workings and philosophy of information systems security (InfoSec) within the business environment, including how to communicate with managers in "their language."

UNDERSTANDING THE BUSINESS ENVIRONMENT

An InfoSec program and organization is not the reason why the business or government agency exists. A business usually provides a service or a product. The business has certain information or systems vital to performing its service and producing its product. The purpose of an InfoSec program, therefore, is to provide *service and support* to the business.

To adequately meet the needs of its customers, it is imperative for the ISSO to understand the company and its business. This includes the following:

1.   Its history,
2.   The products or services it provides,
3.   The environment in which it does business,

4.   The competition it faces,
5.   Its long-range plans,
6.   Its short-range plans,
7.   The cost of doing business,
8.   The value of its product or service.

These are important because the InfoSec program is not a product to be sold in the marketplace, so it brings in no revenue. In fact, the cost of an InfoSec program, no matter how efficient and effective its operation, takes profits away from the business—unless you can prove that the InfoSec program is a value-added service, which financially supports the business and assists in bringing in revenue.

In this globally competitive economy, competition for market shares in the worldwide marketplace is increasing. The ISSO must understand this competition and what the InfoSec program can do to enhance business, thus increasing such things as profits, market shares, and income.

Kenichi Ohmae, in *The Mind of the Strategist,* discusses product or service differentiation in the form of "the strategic three Cs": the corporation, the customers, and the competition (Figure 2.1). Corporations and competitors are differentiated by costs. Customers differentiate between the corporation and competitors by value.

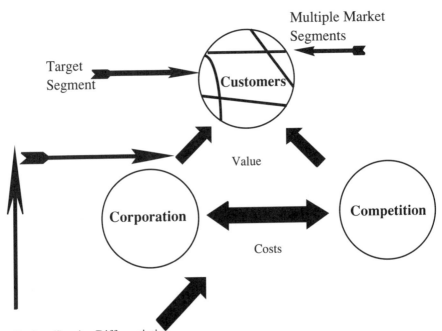

Figure 2.1   Ohmae's three strategic Cs.

Customers will buy products that they want (consider of value), if it is a high-quality product at the right price. Therefore, it is important that the InfoSec program add value to the product and do so at the least cost, for the business to remain competitive in the marketplace. So, treat the InfoSec program as a product that adds value and minimizes cost. It is "your" product, so market it and sell it.

MANAGEMENT RESPONSIBILITIES AND COMMUNICATING WITH MANAGERS

One of the biggest mistakes made by an ISSO is to assume that he or she "owns" the systems and information.The ISSO must remember that the owners of the business, whether it be private ownership or public ownership through the stockholders, make the decisions as to how the business is run. The stockholders do it through their elected members of the company's board of directors. They are the risk takers. Their responsibilities include making decisions relative to company risks.

As an ISSO, you are there because the management believes you have the expertise it needs to protect the business' information systems and the company's information.

All too often, the ISSO gets into a "tail wagging the dog" situation, where the ISSO cannot understand why he or she does not get the needed or wanted support from management. The ISSO must keep in mind that if management did not provide at least some support, he or she would not be employed by the company.

When decisions are made to process, store, or transmit information that goes against the desires of the ISSO, many ISSOs take it personally. Remember, it is not your information!

Of course, depending on your responsibilities and the authority delegated to you by management, you probably will be responsible for making the majority of decisions that involve InfoSec. However, even with that responsibility and authority, the ISSO must gain the support and concurrence of others within the company.

When an InfoSec decision must be made and that decision is outside the purview of the ISSO, you must elevate the final decision to a higher level of management. Although each company's culture and policies will dictate when and how that process will be implemented, the ISSO should be sure to provide complete staff work on which management can base the required decision. In other words, the person making the decision must be provided all the information necessary on which to base the decision. If that information is not provided upper management, the wrong decision could be made, which may jeopardize the protection of the company's information or systems or cause the company to incur unnecessary costs.

If you have done your homework—assessed the risks to the information and systems, the protection alternatives, the costs involved, the benefits involved—and you are in a position to make your recommendations accordingly, then you have done your job.

Prior to elevating the problem and decision to management, you, the ISSO, should be sure that you have addressed the problem by providing management sufficient clear, concise, nontechnical information on which it can base the decision. The following, as a minimum, should be included in that process:

- Identification of the problem;
- Possible problem solutions, including costs and benefits;
- Recommended solution to the problem and the reasons behind it;
- Identification of who should fix the problem (it may not be an InfoSec issue or it may be one outside your authority);
- Consequences of no decision (no action or no decision is always an option, and sometimes the right one).

Whether it is the responsibility of the ISSO to fix the problem or not, the ISSO should follow up. Once the problem is fixed, it is always good to contact the others who were at the meeting where the problem was discussed and the decision made and advise them either verbally or in writing when the corrective action is completed or the project is closed out.

An excellent gesture would be to send a letter of appreciation to those involved in fixing the problem, with appropriate copies to management. This is especially important if the problem was fixed by others outside your organization or staff outside your organization assisted you in fixing the problem.

It is the responsibility of the business management to make the final decision, unless of course it abdicates that responsibility to you. Management, in turn, is held accountable to the owners of the business.

Remember, that managers can make only those decisions related to accepting InfoSec risks for the organizations under their authority. They should not be allowed by the business to make decisions that affect the entire company. If that appears to be occurring, you are obligated to ensure the information is known by the manager as well as upper management. This, of course, is a sensitive matter and must be handled that way.

As a word of caution, some managers will abdicate their management responsibility to the ISSO. As the ISSO, you may be flattered by such a gesture, but beware! You also may be getting set up to take the blame for the consequences. These consequences may be due to a decision that you may not have recommended, in fact one with which you were in total disagreement with management as to the correct course of action to be taken.

The responsibility of business management is a serious one. Under current laws, managers can be held personally responsible and possibly liable for their poor decisions that affect the value of the business. So, your responsibility as a service and support InfoSec professional is to give management the best advice you can. When its decision is made, do your job by supporting that decision and ensuring that the information and systems are protected based on that decision.

Sometimes, in the opinion of the ISSO, management's decision relative to the protection of the information is the wrong one. The ISSO then has several additional choices:

1. Meet with the decision maker in private to try to convince that person about the consequences of the decision and why it may not be the right decision;
2. Appeal the decision to the next level of management;
3. Quit the job or quit the company.

Another word of caution is needed here. Whether the decision is the right or wrong one, the ISSO should document that decision process. The documentation should answer the typical security and investigative questions of who, how, where, when, why, and what.

This is important, not from the standpoint of just another bureaucratic process, but to have a history of InfoSec-related actions taken. Thus, when similar instances occur a year or more from the time of the last decision, it can be used as a precedent-setting decision. This not only would help in making subsequent decisions based on similar instances but also help ensure consistency in the application of InfoSec. Inconsistent InfoSec decisions lead to confusion, which leads to not following sound InfoSec policy and causes increased costs to the business.

If, subsequently, the last decision was found to have unexpected, adverse consequences, then it will help the decision maker not to make the same mistake again (we hope!).

People come and go, but a good historical file will ensure consistency and not having to rely on the memories of people, assuming they were still employed by the company. Consider the following example.

Assume that a major decision had to be made concerning InfoSec and the decision was determined to be that of management. You, as the ISSO, should lead the effort to resolve the issue. You should request a meeting and ensure all the applicable personnel are invited. Then, explain the reason for the meeting, the objective (expected outcome), and the consequences of any decisions made. If you as the ISSO are to keep minutes of the meeting, the documentation of that meeting should include the following:

*   Why the meeting was held;
*   When the meeting was held;
*   Where the meeting was held;
*   Who was at the meeting;

- What information was presented and discussed;
- What decision was reached;
- How did management derive the decision;
- Who made the decision.

The results of the meeting should be signed by someone in management, preferably the one who made the final decision.

You will find that such decisions usually are verbal and most managers do not want to sign any document that will place him or her at risk. So, how do you deal with such issues? Several methods can be used, all of which may cause your position as the ISSO to possibly be questioned; for example, being told "you are not a team player," "you don't understand the big picture," or "you are not a business person so you don't understand the situation."

Even though you have the best interest of the company at heart, that is the basis for your recommendation, and you consider yourself a dedicated and loyal employee, in the eyes of some in management you're not a team player. In other words, you are not on *his* or *her* team.

You soon will find that the position of the ISSO sometimes is risky. Although you do the best professional job that can be done or has been done in the history of the ISSO profession, office politics must be considered. Such non-InfoSec situations often will cause many more problems than the ISSO will come across in dealing with InfoSec issues, hackers, and the like.

If the ISSO does not know about such things as "turf battles" and "protecting rice bowls," the local book store can help. Numerous books will explain how to work and survive in the "jungle" of office politics. You may know InfoSec, but if you do not know office politics, you may not survive—even with the best InfoSec program ever developed. Always remember, "It's a jungle out there." Why is it that way? There are many reasons, but for ISSOs the primary reason is that you "make" people do things that they do not consider part of their job. And, if they do not follow the InfoSec policies and procedures, they could face disciplinary action.

Obviously, as the ISSO, you want to eliminate or at least minimize that type of image—the "cop" image. It is hard work, but you must constantly try to overcome the negativism that people tack onto the ISSO and InfoSec. Some ways of countering that negative image can be found throughout this book.

Many business meetings require that minutes be taken. If so, and you are not responsible for taking the minutes, obtain a copy of the minutes and ensure that your recommendations are noted in them as well as who made what decisions. This is the best method of documenting what went on in the meeting.

If the minutes do not adequately describe what has taken place, such as lacking details of what was presented, the potential risks, or who made the final decision (all crucial pieces of information), annotate the minutes, attach any of your briefing charts, sign and date the minutes, then place them in a file in case you want to use them as a reference at a later date.

Another method that can be used, but is more confrontational, is to send a memo to the manager making the decision in which you document the InfoSec options, costs, benefits, and associated risks. You then conclude with a sentence that states, for example, *"after assessing the risks, I have concluded that the best course of action is option 2."* Leave room for a date and the signature block of the manager you want to sign the document.

The document should be worded professionally and be as nonintimidating to the manager as possible. Even so, in most cases, you may find that you will not get a signed copy returned to you if you send it in the company mail.

This document should be hand carried to the manager and discussed with that person. Imagine yourself in that position. When you put your signature on such a document, there can be no mistake—you made the decision. If something goes wrong, that letter may document that, in retrospect, it was a poor decision. No manager—no one—ever wants to be put in that position. Remember, the manager does not have to sign the InfoSec document. In fact, no matter how it is presented, you will find most managers will find some way *not* to sign the document if there is the slightest chance of being second-guessed later.

Asking a manager to sign such a document, especially if you have voiced disagreement about the decision, should be a last resort and only if you feel so strongly about the decision that you are willing to put your possible raise, possible promotion, or even your employment on the line. So, you better be right and strongly believe that it is worth it. Also, as the ISSO, you must do so as an ISSO professional, a person of integrity and principles. Even so, you may be right but also right out of a job. Well, no one said the job was easy. Being an ISSO professional is a tough job.

CREATING A COMPETITIVE
ADVANTAGE THROUGH INFOSEC

To ensure that the InfoSec program supports the company's business services and products, the ISSO must think of methods, philosophies, and processes that will help the company gain a competitive advantage. Such methods and philosophies should include a team approach: that is, to have the company employees, and especially management, support your InfoSec program.

To help in that endeavor, you should strive to insert, in appropriate company policy documents, policies that can help support your efforts. The following are some examples that may be useful in supporting your

InfoSec program and your quest to assist the company in gaining a competitive advantage through the InfoSec program:

- Managers will ensure a compliant InfoSec program within their organization.
- Managers will develop our customers' trust that their sensitive information will be effectively protected while under our control.
- Managers will employ cost-effective InfoSec systems and strive to help keep the price of our company's services and products as low as possible relative to our competitors.
- Managers will help keep down the company's overhead through effective loss prevention and asset protection processes.
- Managers will minimize the adverse impact of our InfoSec controls on the efficiency of the company's operational functions by working with the InfoSec staff to find the most cost-effective ways of protecting our information assets.
- Managers will proactively find ways to securely and efficiently provide the company's services and products.

THE ISSO AS A BUSINESS MANAGER

The role of the ISSO in managing an InfoSec program is somewhat different from the role of the ISSO as a manager of the company. All company managers have some role to play that applies regardless of the manager's area of responsibility. This also applies to ISSOs in management positions. The following items should be considered for implementation by the ISSO as a manager within the company:

- Comply with all company policies and procedures, including the intent of those policies and procedures.
- Take no action that will give the appearance of violating applicable company policies, procedures, or ethical standards.
- Implement applicable management control systems within the InfoSec organization to ensure the efficient use of resources and effective operations.
- Identify business practices, ethics, and security violations or infractions; conduct inquiries; assess potential damage; direct and take corrective action.
- Communicate with other departments to provide and receive information and guidance for mutual benefit.
- Plan, organize, direct, coordinate, control, report, assess, and refine business activities to achieve quality, cost, schedule, and performance objectives, while retaining responsibility for the results.
- Exercise due diligence to prevent fraud, waste, or abuse.

- Establish and maintain a self-audit process to identify problem areas and take corrective action to eliminate deficiencies.

These items, if made part of the ISSO's philosophy and goals, not only will benefit the company but will assist the ISSO in professionally meeting the InfoSec duties and responsibilities as a valued member of the company's management team. Remember, the InfoSec program is a company program. This means you need help from everyone in the company to ensure its success.

SERVICE, SUPPORT, AND A BUSINESS ORIENTATION

In any business, the ISSO must strive to balance the required user-friendly systems demands of management and users with that of InfoSec. After all, InfoSec, unless it can be proven to be value-added and so at least pay for itself, is a parasite on the profits or at least adversely affects budgets. This will be a factor to consider as you, the ISSO, establish the company's InfoSec program, plans, projects, budgets, and so forth.

The ISSO must remember that the InfoSec program must be service and support oriented. This is of vital importance. The ISSO must understand that the InfoSec program, once it is too costly, outdated, and does not meet the service and support needs of the business or government agency, will be discarded or ignored. Each of these possibilities eventually will lead to the dismissal of the ISSO.

The dismissal of any ISSO has an impact on all ISSOs. The ISSO profession is damaged, as is its professional credibility, and its opportunities to protect vital information for internal and external customers. It is difficult enough, even in today's environment, to "sell" an InfoSec program. Such jobs are harder when one ISSO fails. The failure of an ISSO could be a lesson learned for all ISSOs. Learn not only from your own failures but those of others.

The word of an ISSO's dismissal and failure gets around within the industry and government agencies, making it much more difficult for the ISSO's replacement to develop a professional InfoSec program. You may be that replacement.

As the ISSO, you must constantly update your InfoSec program and its processes. You must continuously look at the changes in society, technology changes, plan for changes, and be prepared to address InfoSec ramifications of the installation of new technology into the business before it is installed, and implement InfoSec measures *before* someone can take advantage of a system vulnerability.

So far, ISSOs for the most part have been in a reactive mode, with little time to be proactive. Put InfoSec defenses in place before they are needed. How to do that will be discussed in the following chapters.

SUMMARY

1. The ISSO must understand the business of his or her company, including its history, products, competition, plans, costs, and product value.
2. The ISSO must understand business, management, and how to communicate with management in its own language—not in "computerese."
3. The ISSO must document major InfoSec decisions to provide a historical file that can be used in the future when considering like situations.
4. The ISSO must also think and act like a business manager of the company.
5. The ISSO must be service and support oriented.

REFERENCES

Ohmae, Kenichi. *The Mind of the Strategist.* Middlesex, England: Penguin Books, 1982.

3

The Corporation Incorporated

CHAPTER OBJECTIVE

The objective of this chapter is to establish and describe a mythical corporation in which the ISSO will work. This method is used to assist the new ISSO by providing a more practical model to help learn how to build an InfoSec program for a company. In other words, a more real-life approach using real scenarios. The scenarios and the actions taken are based on actual situations that can be found in today's business environment.

The reader is encouraged to build an InfoSec program based on The Corporation Incorporated (TCI). This practice not only will assist in focusing on the "how-tos" but can be used when building an interview portfolio (which is discussed in Chapter 5).

One word of caution—the approach used is provided in a simplistic form. Unfortunately, things often are more complex; however, the basics provided are believed to assist the ISSO in the more complex environment.

TCI BACKGROUND INFORMATION

The ISSO must understand TCI's business and processes if a high-quality, cost-effective InfoSec program is to be developed for the firm. Part of that process requires the ISSO to identify those key elements of TCI's history and business that must be considered in developing its InfoSec program.

The following is a summary of TCI's business environment (italics are used to identify the key phrases, which are important elements that the ISSO must take into consideration when building the InfoSec program):

- TCI is a corporation that *manufactures a high-technology* widget. To make these widgets, it uses a *proprietary process* that has evolved over the 12 years TCI has been in business.
- The *proprietary process is the key to TCI's success* as a leader in manufacturing of high-technology widgets. The process costs millions of dollars to develop. The protection of the high-technology widget process is *vital to company survival.*
- TCI does business in an *extremely competitive business* environment. However, based on changes in technology that allow for a more efficient and effective operation through telecommunications and networks, it has found that it must *network with its customers and subcontractors.*
- To maximize the high-technology widget process, it shares its networks with its *subcontractors, who must also use* TCI's *proprietary process.* The subcontractors, *under contractual agreements*, have promised not to use or share TCI's proprietary information with anyone. They also have agreed to protect that information in accordance with the information systems security requirements of their contract with TCI.

KEY ELEMENTS FOR THE ISSO TO CONSIDER

From this background information about TCI, the TCI ISSO should remember some key elements:

1. *TCI is a high-technology corporation:* This means that it uses and is dependent on information systems, a key factor that makes the InfoSec program of vital importance.
2. *It uses a proprietary process:* This means that information relative to the proprietary process is the most valuable information within the TCI, and it probably resides on one or more of TCI's information systems.
3. *The proprietary process is the key to TCI's success and vital to company survival:* The number 1 priority of the InfoSec program must be to ensure that this process receives the highest protection; therefore, it is a top priority for the ISSO to ensure that the current protection mechanisms are in place and adequate. It also means that the location of all information relative to the proprietary process and residing on the information system(s) must be identified and tagged for special access controls and to receive special monitoring and audit trail review.

4. *TCI is in an extremely competitive business:* To the ISSO, this means that the potential for industrial and economic espionage is a factor to consider in establishing the InfoSec program.

5. *TCI is networked with its customers and subcontractors; subcontractors also must use TCI's proprietary process under contractual agreements:* When the ISSO builds the TCI InfoSec Program, the customers' and subcontractors' interfaces to TCI networks must be identified and increased access controls and audit trails must be implemented. This is to ensure that the non-TCI personnel gain access to only that information to which they have been given authorized access, in accordance with contractual requirements.

Further, the ISSO must contact the TCI contracts personnel and determine the contractual requirements relative to the access to the TCI networks and information. If necessary, the ISSO must request additional provisions be made to the contract relative to liability issues and TCI's ISSO authority to evaluate the non-TCI networks InfoSec processes. This is to ensure compliance with the contractual requirements vis-à-vis InfoSec and ensure that the proprietary TCI process information is adequately protected.

GETTING TO KNOW TCI

The new ISSO should walk around the entire company, see how widgets are made, see what processes are used to make the widgets, AND watch the process from beginning to end. The ISSO should know as much as possible about the company. It is very important that the ISSO understand the inner workings of the company.

Unfortunately, many new ISSOs sit through a general orientation given to new employees, learn some general information about the company, then go to their office. They start working and may not see how the company actually operates or makes widgets. They never meet the other people who play a role in InfoSec. These include the people using automated systems on the factory floor, human resources personnel, quality control personnel, auditors, procurement personnel, contracts personnel, and in-house subcontractors and other non-TCI employees.

When asked why they do not walk around the plant or understand the company processes, the normal reply is, "I don't have the time. I'm too busy 'putting out fires.' " The answer to that dilemma is this: Take a time management course, manage your time better, and make the time.

An ISSO cannot provide a service- and support-oriented InfoSec program without understanding the company, its culture, and how its products are made. If you want to spend your time "putting out fires," do it right—join the fire department because you will not be a successful ISSO.

The ISSO should know how the manufacturing process takes place, how manufacturing is supported by other company elements, how employees use the computers and telecommunications systems, what problems they have doing their jobs because of InfoSec constraints, and whether or not they even follow the InfoSec policies and procedures.

All the InfoSec policies and procedures neatly typed and placed in binders are ignored if they get in the way of employees fulfilling their primary functions. The ISSO cannot see this from one office or cubicle. The ISSO can find this out only by walking around the areas where the people work and actually use information systems.

TCI'S STRATEGIC BUSINESS PLAN

TCI has developed a proprietary Strategic Business Plan. The plan describes TCI's strategy for maintaining its competitive edge in the manufacture of high-technology widgets. That plan sets the baseline and the direction that TCI will follow for the next seven years. It is considered TCI's long-range plan. Management decided that any plan longer than seven years was not feasible, due to the rapidly changing environment brought on by technology and TCI's competitive business environment.

The Strategic Business Plan sets forth the following:

1.   The expected annual earnings for the next seven years;
2.   The market-share percentage goals on an annual basis;
3.   The future process modernization projects based on expected technology changes of faster, cheaper, and more powerful computers, telecommunications systems, and robotics;
4.   TCI expansion goals;
5.   TCI's acquisition of some current subcontractors and competitive companies.

The Strategic Business Plan also calls for a mature InfoSec program that can protect TCI's information while allowing access to its networks by its international and national customers, subcontractors, and suppliers. In addition, the InfoSec program is expected to be capable of supporting the integration of new hardware, software, networks, and the like while maintaining the required level of InfoSec with no impact on schedules or costs.

Key Elements of TCI's Strategic Business
Plan That the ISSO Should Consider

The ISSO must ensure that the Strategic Business Plan, which also resides on the TCI networks, is protected at a priority level second only to the proprietary processes. Protection of this information is vital to the future of TCI. Its release to those without the need-to-know authorization could cause it to fall into the hands of TCI's competitors. That would jeopardize TCI's competitive edge and its leadership position in the widget business.

The ISSO probably will find that the information making up the Strategic Business Plan is scattered throughout the company. The consolidation of all that information into one file, the TCI Strategic Business Plan file, makes it a tempting target for someone who wants to use that information to his or her advantage and at a cost to TCI.

Centralized information can be protected more cost effectively. However, that consolidation has drawbacks vis-à-vis convenient use by authorized employees in this era of distributed systems. Also, it becomes a more visible target for attack. So, consider that some benefits may accrue from nonconsolidation of information.

Another reason why the ISSO must understand the TCI Strategic Business Plan is that the InfoSec program must include an InfoSec Strategic Business Plan that provides the strategies necessary to support the TCI plan.

TACTICAL BUSINESS PLAN

TCI also has a proprietary Tactical Business Plan. The Tactical Business Plan, which is a three-year plan, sets more definitive goals, objectives, and tasks. The Tactical Business Plan is the short-range plan used to support TCI's Strategic Business Plan. TCI's successful implementation and completion of its projects is a critical element in meeting the firm's goals and objectives.

The Tactical Business Plan also calls for the *completion* of an InfoSec program that can protect TCI's information while allowing access to its networks by its international and national customers, subcontractors, and suppliers. In addition, the program is expected to be able to integrate new hardware, software, networks, and the like with a *minimal* impact on schedules or costs.

Key Elements of TCI's Tactical Business Plan That the ISSO Should Consider

The TCI Tactical Business Plan also must be protected in a fashion similar to the TCI Strategic Business Plan. However, a less secure environment may be possible, because it is a support plan that provides the tactics to support the Strategic Business Plan.

The ISSO always must remember that information is time sensitive; that is, its value is time dependent. Therefore, compromise of the TCI Tactical Business Plan would not cause as much damage to TCI as compromise of the TCI Strategic Business Plan. Therefore, the protection requirements could be less stringent and less costly. This is a key factor in protecting any information: *It should be protected using only those methods necessary and only for the time period required, based on the value of that information.* The TCI InfoSec Program must contain processes to re-evaluate the protection mechanisms used to protect information so that it is protected for only the period required.

As was true with the TCI Strategic Business Plan, the ISSO must understand the TCI Tactical Business Plan, because an InfoSec Tactical Business Plan must be developed to integrate InfoSec service and support into the tactical plan. The InfoSec Tactical Business Plan should identify the goals, objectives, and tactics necessary to support the TCI Tactical Business Plan.

A key point that should not be overlooked can be found by comparing portions of the TCI Strategic and Tactical Business Plans. The TCI Strategic Business Plan stated that, "In addition, it is expected that the InfoSec program will be capable of supporting the integration of new hardware, software, networks, and the like while maintaining the required level of InfoSec with no impact on schedules or costs." The TCI Tactical Business Plan states that, "In addition, the program is expected to be able to integrate new hardware, software, networks, and the like with a *minimal* impact on schedules or costs."

The interpretation can be made that the ISSO has three years to establish an InfoSec program with minimal impact to schedules and costs. After that three year period, it is expected that the InfoSec program will have no impact on schedules or costs. As the new ISSO, you must determine if that goal of zero impact is possible. (Hint: There always will be some impact; the goal should be to minimize that impact.)

As the new ISSO, this potential conflict immediately should be brought to the attention of upper management for clarification and interpretation. The apparent conflict may have been caused by a poor choice of words. However, the TCI management may have meant what was said. It then is up to you to meet that objective or have the sentence clarified and changed.

TCI'S ANNUAL BUSINESS PLAN

TCI further has a proprietary annual plan that sets forth its goals and objectives for the year. This plan defines the specific projects to be implemented and completed by the end of the year. The successful completion of these projects will contribute to the success of TCI's Tactical and Strategic Business Plans.

TCI's Annual Plan calls for hiring an ISSO to establish an InfoSec program that can provide for the protection of TCI's information and systems while allowing access to its networks by its customers, subcontractors, and suppliers.

The ISSO also will be responsible for forming and managing an InfoSec organization. The ISSO will report to the vice president of the Information Technology Management (ITM) Department, who also is TCI's corporate information officer (CIO). The CIO reports to the corporate executive officer (CEO).

It should be noted that TCI's executive management agreed that an ISSO position should be established and the ISSO hired should establish TCI's InfoSec program and establish and manage the InfoSec organization. However, there was not complete agreement as to whom, in TCI, the ISSO reported.

Some members of TCI's executive management suggested the CIO; others suggested that the ISSO report to the Director of Security. They argued that placing the ISSO in the information systems organization was like asking the fox to watch the henhouse. They feared that information protection would be compromised in favor of more open systems and less impact on systems performance.

Other members of executive management recommended that the ISSO report to the director of auditing. However, the director of auditing advised that the Auditing Department was responsible strictly for determining TCI's compliance with applicable state, federal, and international laws and company policies and procedures. The Director felt that the auditors' limited scope and functions would adversely limit the ISSO in establishing and managing an InfoSec program.

This Director also argued that it may be a conflict of interest for the ISSO to establish InfoSec policies and procedures, albeit with management support and approval, while having another part of that organization (the audit group) determine not only compliance with the InfoSec policies and procedures but also their adequacy.

The Director of Security advised that having the ISSO and the InfoSec organization in his department might provide the appearance of more objectivity. However, this Director knew very little about computers and would not be in a position to adequately manage such a function. The Director did state that any issues relative to the physical security of the company assets such as computers should be brought to the attention of his staff.

Therefore, the management decided that the ISSO position and organization should be established within the ITM department. Apparently, no one else seemed to want to be responsible for the function.

The new ISSO's understanding of how this position ended up where it did provides some clue as to the feelings and inner workings of TCI's management vis-à-vis the ISSO and the InfoSec program. This information will be useful when the ISSO begins to establish TCI's InfoSec program and when the ISSO requests support from these directors. It also provides the ISSO some insight as to what type of support he or she might receive from these directors.

For example, the physical security of the information systems apparently is under the purview of the Director of Security. It would not be wise for the new ISSO to attempt to place that function under the authority and responsibility of the InfoSec organization. At the same time, the ISSO undoubtedly can get the cooperation, and probably support, of the Director of Security on matters dealing with the physical protection of the information systems.

Another example of the use of such information is this: Knowing that no major, logical department within TCI wanted the InfoSec responsibility could be leveraged. This means that those department heads may not mind supporting the InfoSec program but want little responsibility for that effort. This provides the ISSO the possibility of being a strong leader without concern that the directors identified would want to absorb some of the InfoSec functions into their departments. Therefore, a more centralized, ISSO-directed InfoSec program probably can be established.

Furthermore, the Director of Auditing would clearly support the InfoSec program from a compliance audit standpoint but probably would not want to join a TCI team with the responsibility for writing the new InfoSec policies and procedures. The ISSO must keep this in mind when deciding how to establish InfoSec policies and procedures: what departments should be involved in what part of that development process and so on.

Key Elements of TCI's Annual Business Plan That the ISSO Should Consider

Like the TCI Strategic and Tactical Business Plans, the TCI Annual Business Plan must be protected. Because, as the name states, the TCI Annual Business Plan is developed every year, its protection can be less than the other plans. However, the protection mechanisms used should take into consideration those mechanisms used to protect the TCI Strategic and Tactical Business Plans.

If the other two plans are stored on-line in conjunction with the Annual Business Plan, this means that the Annual Business Plan probably would need no additional protection because the higher level of protection provided the other two plans would suffice for protecting the Annual Business Plan, too.

And, as noted already, the ISSO must also develop an InfoSec Annual Plan or Annual Business Plan. That plan must include the goals, objectives, and projects that will support the goals and objectives of TCI's Annual Business Plan.

INFOSEC PROGRAM PLANNING

The main philosophy running through this chapter should be obvious: As part of a service and support organization, the TCI InfoSec program must include plans that support the business plans of the company.

The ISSO should be able to map each major business goal and objective of each plan to key InfoSec projects and functions. When writing the applicable InfoSec plans, the ISSO also will be able to see which functions are not being supported. This may not be a problem. However, the mapping will allow the ISSO to identify areas where required support for the plans has not been identified in the ISSO's plans. The ISSO then can add additional tasks where increased InfoSec program support is needed. An additional benefit of following this procedure is to be able to show management how the InfoSec program is supporting the business.

When mapping the InfoSec plans to the business plans, summarize the goals, as they will be easier to map.

SUMMARY

1. The fictitious corporation, TCI, can be used by the reader to build an InfoSec program that later can be used as part of an interview portfolio and also to build or improve an InfoSec program for a corporation.
2. Most corporations set their goals and objectives in planning documents such as strategic, tactical, and annual business plans. These plans are key documents for the ISSO to use to determine the corporation's future directions.
3. These plans also are key documents to use to determine what is expected from the ISSO and the InfoSec program.
4. The plans also should be used as the basis for writing service and support InfoSec plans and as separate documents or as sections that are integrated into the identified corporate planning documents.
5. The decision process of the TCI executive management in determining in which department the ISSO and the InfoSec organization belongs provides key information, which should be used by the ISSO in establishing the InfoSec program and organization.

4

ISSO Career Development

CHAPTER OBJECTIVE

The objective of this chapter is to provide the person seeking to be an ISSO, or a current ISSO, a career development plan to be used to prepare for increased responsibilities, promotions, and other ISSO positions.

CAREER DEVELOPMENT PLANNING

Whether you want to become an ISSO or are an ISSO, you should have a career development plan. That plan is similar to any other project plan. That is, it has stated objectives, milestones, and starting and ending dates. The starting time is now and the ending date is the date of your planned retirement. Remember, it is never too early or to late to begin planning your ISSO career and developing the career plan that will challenge you to reach your full potential. The sooner you start, the more likely you are to succeed in meeting your goals and objectives before your retirement. After all, you do not want to spend your retired time thinking about what may have been.

Assume that you enjoy the profession of InfoSec and being an ISSO. This is your chosen profession, your career. Therefore, you should strive to be the best ISSO in the business, and the one most eligible to fill any ISSO position. This takes hard work and dedication.

So, let us put together an ISSO career development plan outline. You can add the specifics that apply to you. Also, assume you are new to the field and you are starting with no InfoSec experience whatsoever.

The basic categories at the foundation for your career development are (1) those categories that make up the ISSO profession, (2) the education and training required for each position, (3) the experience needed for each position, and (4) certification.

ISSO CAREER FIELD JOB DESCRIPTIONS
AND QUALIFICATIONS

For the person putting together a personal career development program or plan, it is important to know the basic positions available within the ISSO career field. The job family provides a gradual progression through an ISSO career beginning with little or no education and experience, emphasizing the technical career development. The management career field generally follows the common management job family; therefore, it is not addressed here. In addition, in most corporations, the InfoSec management position(s) within the corporation are very limited—actually, limited to one. Career growth is likely to be achieved by changing corporations or government agencies.

An ISSO or InfoSec job family follows. The titles, position summaries, functional descriptions, and qualifications are based on actual ISSO job families found in several InfoSec organizations of international corporations. (Detailed job descriptions and responsibilities will be found in Chapter 8.)

1. *Title:* Systems Security Administrator.
    Position Summary: Provide all technical administrative support to the InfoSec organization staff, including filing, typing reports, word processing, developing related spreadsheets, databases, and text/graphic presentations, related analysis, and report development.
    Functions: Administration.
    Education and Experience Requirements: High school diploma, one year of InfoSec administrative experience or two years of clerical experience. Must type at least 60 words per minute.
    Note: This position, although administrative, provides an opportunity to be employed in an InfoSec organization and, more important, the opportunity to learn InfoSec. The potential for advancement to an InfoSec professional position should be possible. That determination should be made prior to the acceptance of the position by one who desires an InfoSec career.
2. *Title:* Systems Security Analyst, Associate.
    Position Summary: Assist and support the InfoSec organization's staff in ensuring all applicable customers, TCI, and subcontractor basic InfoSec requirements are met.

Functions: Users and systems administration and audit report analyses.
Education and Experience Requirements: Bachelor's degree in a related field or at least six years of experience.

3. *Title:* Systems Security Analyst.
   Position Summary: Identify, schedule, administer, and perform assigned technical InfoSec analyses functions to ensure that all applicable customers, TCI, and subcontractor InfoSec requirements are met.
   Functions: Users and systems administration and audit report analyses.
   Education and Experience Requirements: Bachelor's degree in a related field and two years of related experience or a total of eight years of related experience.

4. *Title:* Systems Security Analyst, Senior.
   Position Summary: Identify, evaluate, conduct, schedule, and lead technical InfoSec analysis functions to ensure that all applicable customers, TCI, and subcontractor InfoSec requirements are met.
   Functions: User and systems administration, audit report analyses, and systems security tests and evaluations.
   Education and Experience Requirements: Bachelor's degree in a related field and 4 years of related experience or a total of 10 years of related experience.

5. *Title:* Systems Security Analyst, Specialist.
   Position Summary: Act as technical InfoSec advisor, focal point, and leader to ensure all InfoSec functions are meeting all applicable customers, TCI, and subcontractor InfoSec requirements, as well as develop and administer applicable InfoSec programs.
   Functions: User and systems administration, audit report analyses, systems security tests and evaluations, InfoSec awareness program, noncompliance inquiries, InfoSec requirements, disaster recovery and contingency planning, software evaluation, security software maintenance and enhancement, and network security.
   Education and Experience Requirements: Bachelor's degree in a related field and 6 years of related experience or a total of 12 years of related experience.

6. *Title:* Systems Security Engineer.
   Position Summary: Act as technical InfoSec management consultant, focal point, and project leader for InfoSec functions and programs developed to ensure that all applicable customers, TCI, and subcontractor InfoSec requirements are met.
   Functions: User and systems administration; audit report analyses; systems security tests and evaluations; InfoSec awareness program; noncompliance inquiries; InfoSec requirements; disaster recovery and contingency planning; software evaluation, security software maintenance, enhancements, and development; network security; project leading.

Education and Experience Requirements: Bachelor's degree in a related field and 10 years of related experience or a total of 16 years of related experience.

EDUCATION

Most ISSOs have used either of these two approaches:

1. They began with a technical education, such as a degree or degrees in computer science, mathematics, or telecommunications. Because of their degree, or probably some related InfoSec experience, they were chosen or volunteered to be the company's ISSO.
2. They began with a general degree, such as in business, security, criminal justice, or liberal arts, and eventually, somehow, found themselves in the ISSO position. Once in that position, they decided to stay in the ISSO profession.

In today's environment, a college degree with a major in computer science or telecommunications is one of the best ways to start an ISSO career. An alternative is to major in InfoSec. As colleges and universities see the demand for such subjects, they will offer InfoSec courses and programs. As the need for InfoSec grows, more universities and colleges will begin to offer majors in InfoSec.

An alternative to a college or university is a technical school that offers InfoSec-related specialized programs in various aspects of the computer and telecommunications functions. This training usually offers hands-on experience and may provide a faster avenue into the ISSO profession. Also, many colleges and universities offer certificates in a specialized ISSO-related field such as local area networks or telecommunications. These courses also can be applied to the degree program, but check the college or university to be sure. Those that choose the technical training path still should pursue a college degree, which will enhance promotion opportunities in the ISSO profession.

Education, whether technical or academic, provides the future ISSO with an opportunity for an ISSO position. Notice that I said *opportunity* for a position. In today's business environment, the certification or degree will provide you only the opportunity for a possible interview. As you probably have already discovered, there is growing competition for these positions. As the profession grows in importance, that competition is expected to increase.

In today's marketplace, the need for experience coupled with advanced degrees and certifications has increased to the point where all your education, experience, and certification get you through only the first resume-filtering process. *The interview will get you the job.*

CONFERENCES, TRAINING, AND NETWORKING

To prepare yourself for an ISSO position, try to complement your education with as much training as possible. Numerous associations, consultants, and companies provide training classes, workshops, and conferences that cover the entire field of InfoSec. Although none is very cheap—of course, that is relative—they provide opportunities to gain first-hand knowledge of many InfoSec topics. These InfoSec topics range from the administrative, nontechnical aspects of InfoSec to the technical. The following lists are of conference sessions and workshops from a typical InfoSec conference (an InfoSec Association/MIS Institute conference).

Conference Sessions

1. Public Key Infrastructures,
2. Wireless and Cellular Phone Fraud,
3. E-Cash Security,
4. Securing Sun Networks,
5. Developing and Implementing an Internet Security Policy,
6. Single Sign-On,
7. Best Practices for Information Security,
8. Using HP OpenView as a Security and Audit Tool,
9. Controlling Dial-up Security,
10. Securing Sybase and SQL Server,
11. Security Behind the Firewall: UNIX-TCP/IP,
12. Security and Audit of JAVA and ActiveX,
13. Kerberos, SESAME, and Other Third-Party Products,
14. Handling Security Incidents,
15. Crypto APIs,
16. Securing the NetWare-TCP/IP Interface,
17. Open Systems Security Management,
18. Telecommuting Security,
19. Hacker Tools and Techniques,
20. Protecting and Auditing Distributed Oracle Databases,
21. HP/UX Security,
22. Enterprise Network Security,
23. The Legal Aspects of Internet Connections,
24. Entrust, PGP, and Other Crypto Software,
25. Configuring and Securing Windows NT Web Servers,
26. Testing Firewalls and Other Types of Barrier Security,
27. Securing Windows NT in a TCP/IP Network,
28. Workstation Security,

29. Building a Security Awareness Program,
30. Decentralizing Security Administration,
31. Security and Audit Tools for Non-UNIX Systems,
32. Virtual Private Networks,
33. Securing Application Design,
34. Securing OpenVMS,
35. Client-Side Security: Securing the Browser,
36. E-Mail Security,
37. AIX Security and Audit,
38. The Web as a Distributed Computing Environment,
39. Security Mechanisms for Electronic Commerce,
40. Navigating the Internet for Audit and Security,
41. Intranet Security,
42. Virus Protection,
43. NT Enterprise Security,
44. Information Warfare and the ISSO.

Optional Workshops

1. Policy Writing,
2. Building Secure Firewalls,
3. Introduction to TCP/IP Network Security,
4. Advanced UNIX Administration,
5. Introduction to Web Security and Audit,
6. Disaster Recovery Planning,
7. Building a Business-Oriented InfoSec Program,
8. Auditing Your Internet Connection,
9. Windows NT Security and Audit,
10. Developing an Enterprise Security Architecture.

These training courses and workshops also give you the opportunity to find out what works and what does not work, which will come in handy some day when you become an ISSO. You will not have to learn the hard way—by experience. Do not concern yourself with the *"not-invented-here-syndrome."* Learn from the mistakes of others and apply what will work for you, your career, and your InfoSec program.

Remember, it is not where you get your information or methodology that counts, it is whether you apply it successfully. Your company is interested in results. So, *be results oriented.*

Prior to attending any conference or workshop that provides a choice of courses on various topics, you should know what up-to-date information you are lacking. Then, be sure to attend those courses that provide that information. Also, be sure to ask questions. The purpose of the courses are to exchange information and learn from each other.

To determine on what InfoSec courses and knowledge areas you should concentrate while at the conference or what training you require, use the tables in Figures 4.1 and 4.2. Rate your experience or knowledge using either a scale from 1 to 5 or high, medium, and low. Be honest and objective, because if not, you are only cheating yourself. After you complete that section, sequentially number the training you need in a priority order. Obviously, the lower your current knowledge rating, the higher you should rank the type of training needed and vice versa.

Networking

While at the conference or training course, be sure to get a list of the participants, which normally is available. Using the list of participants, you should make it a point to identify and seek out those who work in the government agency or business you would like to target for employment. For example, some ISSOs like to work in the banking and finance business, others in manufacturing, aerospace, accounting firms, and so on.

During the breaks, find these people. Everyone is given a badge that normally contains their name and the business or government agency they work for. So, it should not be that difficult to find people. Go through the crowds, find the person, introduce yourself, and ask your questions. You will find that you may not be the only one puzzled by a new technology or how to apply InfoSec to a particular system configuration.

Management Topics	Current Knowledge	Learning Priority
Time Management		
Project Management		
Communicating with Others		
Managing People		
Planning		
Directing		
Controlling		
Budgeting		
Managerial Finance		
Managerial Accounting		
Marketing		

Figure 4.1 A table to determine current ISSO management strengths and weaknesses and identify training needs.

Technical Topics	Current Knowledge	Learning Priority
InfoSec Policies & Processes		
Sys. Authorization & Access Control		
Systems Security		
Risk Assessment		
Communications Security		
Physical & Environmental Security		
Security Awareness & Training		
Contingency Planning		
Disaster Recovery		
Application Security		

Figure 4.2   A table to determine current ISSO technical strengths and weaknesses and identify training needs.

Many attendees are strangers on the first day of these events but become professional friends by the time the conference ends. Then, it is a matter of continuous networking (keeping in touch by e-mail, fax, or telephone) and discussing what is going on in the profession, in industry, or whatever.

A word of caution is appropriate: If you find someone who is not interested in discussing InfoSec with you or wants you to pay for that information to you (yes, it does happen on occasion), do not feel bad. Do not be embarrassed or discouraged. Find others more professional. Like any other profession, the ISSO profession includes some *un*professional people.

During each session, sit with someone you have not met before and learn what he or she does, at what company, and so on. With each break and at each luncheon or dinner, try to meet someone new. Remember your objective is to meet people who will share InfoSec information with you, people you can contact at a later date to find out about job opportunities, how to fix a particular problem, and the like.

When you attend these conferences, training sessions, and association meetings, be sure to bring plenty of business cards—and do not be shy. Ask others for their cards. If you have no card, get some printed, even if the card lists only your name, home address, telephone number, fax number, and e-mail address. You often find that you can get 500 business cards for as little as $30, a small investment when considering the person with your card may some day call you and tell you of a great, new ISSO position in some company—one that was "made" for you.

If you hand out your card and someone asks you what you do, be honest. If you are unemployed, employed in a non-ISSO position, or a student, just say so. Tell the person you really enjoy the ISSO profession and are trying very hard to get into it. You may be surprised at the response and how people will try to help you.

One of the greatest benefits of attending conferences and chapter meetings of InfoSec-related associations is the opportunity to network with those in the profession. This is the best way to find out what the ISSOs in government agencies and businesses are doing in the InfoSec arena. They are also some of the best sources of information as to what ISSO positions are opening at what company or government agency.

Remember, few of the ISSO positions are advertised in the newspapers. Those that are usually are advertised because the company did not want to hire an employment firm to fill the position, or maybe the position called for $100,000 worth of experience for $25,000.

If you are new to the ISSO profession, you may have to apply for such a position and hope that, although you lack all the experience and education the firm desires, you are the best candidate that has applied for the position.There is nothing wrong with "buying in" to the position by accepting the lower than expected salary. It is a start, and once you have two or three years of experience, you have a better opportunity to get a better ISSO position and command a higher salary. Who knows, your company may give you a counteroffer if you have done a great job for it.

Another great tool for networking is the Internet. By obtaining the names and e-mail addresses of people you meet at conferences, association meetings, and the like, you can begin a dialogue with those in the profession.

THE INTERNET

A rapidly growing source of InfoSec information is the Internet. Many groups are out on the Internet that discuss both general and specific InfoSec issues. There are many government sites, business sites, sites managed by InfoSec product suppliers, and even easy-to-find hacker sites.

All the Internet sites provide information that can help you learn about InfoSec positions, problems, solutions to those problems, techniques for breaking into systems, and so forth. All this information is available just by doing an Internet search.

If you do not have Internet access, subscribing to an Internet service provider should be your number 1 goal. It is almost impossible to be an ISSO professional today without having an Internet account and Internet address for electronic mail (e-mail).

You probably will find that your major problem will not be finding useful InfoSec information on the Internet but finding so much useful information that you cannot keep up with all of it. Do not feel bad, no one can. Using your completed self-evaluation knowledge tables (Figures 4.1 and 4.2), concentrate your information search in those areas where you are weakest. Then, if you have time, research and review the other InfoSec documents.

A good way of ensuring that you do the research and review is to

1. Set up your Internet web sites through the use of your Internet browser's "Bookmarks." That way, you need not continually search for the sites that have the best information relative to your InfoSec needs.
2. Set up a specific time each day when you can and do commit at least one hour to read and learn from the material in your personal library, text books, Internet sites, and so forth.

To be successful, of course, you must have self-discipline and good study habits. However, you will find that the rewards of new InfoSec knowledge gained through such study habits, as well as successfully applying those newly learned techniques, will be well worth your efforts.

TRADE JOURNAL AND MAGAZINE TRAINING

Another overlooked and usually free source of information is the technology trade journals and magazines. Such journals and magazines contain articles about the latest technologies and problems with this or that software; and more and more contain InfoSec-related articles. All this information will help you stay abreast of the technology and the related security issues.

Those trade journals related to data communications, telecommunications, InfoSec, disaster recovery and contingency planning, information news, and so forth are especially useful. Many such journals can be found on the Internet, making the search and the training convenient and, best of all, at no cost but your time.

You must stay up-to-date on these changes. Once mainframe computer experience and access control software experience was needed. Now, you read about TCP/IP, UNIX, web pages, and the like.If you stay in this profession, be prepared to learn the rest of your professional life.

If you do not keep current in the technology, the technology will probably make you obsolete in less than five years.

EXPERIENCE

Many people filling ISSO positions today did not start out to be an ISSO. For many, the ISSO did not exist when they began their journey in InfoSec.

As with anyone entering a profession, the challenges are many. How does one become an ISSO if the company or government agency wants a person with experience? Inexperienced candidates seem to never have the chance to gain that experience—the typical "catch-22" situation. However, this is the same for all professions.

Many excellent books on the market address the issues of job hunting and how to gain experience. I will not address the subject in any great level of detail in this book. Suffice it to say, the reader can find many of these books at the local library, on-line through Internet, and at a local bookstore. The important point is to get several books and articles and use them to your advantage.

The best approach to take is to get experience anywhere and in any way you can. Many people fall into the trap of thinking that they can gain the InfoSec experience they need only by being employed in the profession. If you can do that, great! However, what if you cannot?

There are several other ways to gain related experience. Many schools, ranging from elementary and universities to senior associations, may need some type of help related to information systems: So, volunteer. You can volunteer to help organizations with their computer needs. Sometimes, the help needed may be as simple as helping to load new software on a microcomputer or installing a new piece of computer hardware.

While you are doing volunteer work, also volunteer to set up some access controls, audits trails. Maybe you can even volunteer to periodically review the audit trails to ensure that the systems are not being abused or used for unauthorized purposes.

The main point is that it is a win-win situation.The organizations get the help they need while you gain the experience you need.You may be surprised to learn that many small companies also would greatly appreciate your volunteered assistance.

You can find such work by contacting various charitable organizations, discussing it with members of your church, city council members, local chamber of commerce, business associations, and friends who already volunteer. Who knows, you may find that your volunteer work leads to consulting work or a permanent position.

So, volunteer. You will not only help yourself but, maybe more important, others in need, your community, and your chosen profession.

CERTIFICATION

What is meant by *certification*? For our purposes, *certification* means that, based on your experience, education, and successfully passing a test, generally given by some InfoSec or related association, you are certified to have the basic knowledge and ability to meet the criteria for certifying you as a professional or expert in a particular field.

The word *expert* may not be correct because, in the InfoSec business, technology and systems vulnerabilities change rapidly, making it impossible for anyone to be an expert for long. So, to be more exact, by being certified, you are considered to have the *expertise* in the particular field.

Several certifications are directly related to the position of an ISSO. A professional ISSO should have the basic knowledge of some, if not all, of these ISSO-related certifications.

The certification directly related to the professional ISSO is the *Certified Information Systems Security Professional* (CISSP) designation. The CISSP is awarded by the International Information Systems Security Certification Consortium (ISC). The (ISC2) was started by members of several InfoSec-related associations and data processing management associations, in the United States and Canada.

The CISSP designation was first awarded about 1992 by "grandfathering in" a select group of InfoSec professionals who met the minimum criteria of five years of direct experience and 36 months of substitute experience for a total of at least 96 months, or eight years, of experience in the InfoSec profession.

Many of these individuals then attended a training class on how to write test questions and volunteered to write multiple choice test questions. The questions were compiled into categories and became the CISSP certification examination. The individual questions and answers had to meet a stringent criteria to ensure fairness. In other words, no trick questions. The idea is to determine if the individual taking the test has the basic knowledge necessary to be certified as a CISSP.

The CISSP examination is given at several locations in the United States, usually coinciding with one of the sponsoring association's annual conferences. To be eligible for the examination, an individual must have at least three years of ISSO-related experience. Once certified, the CISSP must be recertified every three years by obtaining a minimum of 120 CPE points.

The examination is made up of multiple choice questions in the following categories:

1. InfoSec Policies, Procedures, and Standards;
2. System Authorization and Access Control;
3. System Security;
4. Information Security Management;
5. Risk Management;
6. Communications Security;
7. Physical and Environmental Security;
8. Security Awareness and Training;
9. Contingency Planning;
10. Applications Security.

After completing the examination, the candidate is notified whether or not he or she has passed the test. If not, the candidate may retake the test at any time. A candidate who successfully passes the examination is sent a certificate attesting to his or her certification and awarded the title *Certified Information Systems Security Professional.*

For more information about the CISSP, you can contact ISC2 by e-mail at ISC2_@compuserve.com;[1] by fax at 508-842-6461; or by mail at ISC2, Suite 1000, 255 Park Ave., Worcester, MA, 01609.

Several other associations certify professionals in InfoSec-related professions:

- Certified Information Systems Auditors (CISA). Information about CISA can be found on the InfoSec and Audit (ISACA) Internet web site: *http://www.securityserver.com/company/$isaca.htm.*
- Certified Protection Professional (CPP). The CPP is sponsored by the American Society for Industrial Security (ASIS). Information about the CPP can be found on the ASIS web site: *http://www.asisonline.org.*
- Certified Fraud Examiner (CFE). The CFE is sponsored by the Association of Certified Fraud Examiners (ACFE). Information about the CFE can be found on the ACFE web site: *http://www.acfe.org.*

ASSOCIATIONS

As a professional ISSO, you should become a member and take part in one or more of several associations related to InfoSec. These include the Computer Security Institute (CSI), the Information Systems Security Association (ISSA), and the International Computer Security Association (ICSA), in addition to the ACFE, ASIS, and ISACA already mentioned.

Like any other associations, you get out of them only what you are willing to put into them. These associations usually have local chapter meetings. You should attend these meeting, take part in them, volunteer to help, and when you are ready to lead, run for office.

Several of the associations also sponsor annual international conferences. These conferences give the ISSO the opportunity to meet other ISSO professionals and share problems and solutions on an international scale.

Active participation in your chosen professional associations is not only required of a true ISSO professional but provides you the opportunity to learn new InfoSec methods, handle new problems, and network with your peers.

You will find that, by investing your time in these associations, you are rewarded in many ways. By supporting your chosen association(s), you help support your profession and make it better.

---

[1] The e-mail addresses and web sites may change over time. However, using your Internet search engine you should be able to easily find the new address.

THE PERSONAL CAREER
DEVELOPMENT PROJECT PLAN

It is strange that ISSO professionals will develop, implement, and manage InfoSec programs and projects for their company or government agency, but never think of putting together a project plan for their own careers.

Most ISSOs seem to take the best position they can find and try to either stay in that position until they retire, move to a non-ISSO position, or continue to move on to new ISSO positions without any real plan. Then, one day, they find they were never able to get the type of ISSO position that they had wanted for much of their career. They then retire and think of what they had accomplished and what could have been.

By developing your own, personal career development plan, you will be in a better position to be the most eligible person for that ISSO job you wanted for so long. You will be in a better position to control your own ISSO career.

Your ISSO career plan's objective is up to you, and even though you are successful in preparing for the next promotion or new ISSO position, you may not get it. We live in an imperfect world, where prejudices of all kinds reside and office politics takes precedent over other factors, so you may not get the position you wanted—this time. Do not be discouraged. Still prepare yourself, as you will never know when your time will come.

How do you prepare for that next ISSO opportunity or *the* ISSO position? Begin with your objective. Assume you are willing to work for a company or government agency until you are 55 years old. At that time, you want to have acquired a certain salary, be in a position to manage the InfoSec program of a major international organization or major government agency and generally enjoy the perks that come with that position.

At age 55, and after an illustrious career as a well-known ISSO, you want to be an InfoSec consultant until you are 62 years old. At that time, you decide to write your memoirs, go golfing, go fishing, maybe teach a little, but generally enjoy the good life of retirement. Well, before you pack your retirement bags, look at what it takes to meet your objectives and their associated milestones.

To begin, you must do research. Many InfoSec magazines and trade journals are available through the InfoSec associations, by free subscription, and, as always, there is the Internet. You want to know the following:

1. What ISSO positions are available in business or government agencies and where?
2. What minimum education is required for those positions?
3. What minimum years of experience are required for those positions?

4.   What type of agencies or businesses require what type of ISSO profes-
     sionals?
5.   What are the job descriptions for each of those ISSO positions?

In developing your plan, begin with your present position and use
the job family described in the beginning of this chapter to determine your
goals and the education, training, and experience you need to attain them.
After determining what you need, put together a project plan with tasks
and dates for accomplishment of those tasks. Upon completion of that
project, search for the position that meets your new qualifications and
begin marketing yourself for that position.

For example, using the job descriptions noted in the beginning of this
chapter and the completed technical matrix of Figure 4.2, list those positions beginning with the position that most closely describes your current
ISSO function. If you are not an ISSO, then begin with the first position,
the administrative position, if you have the capabilities noted for that position. If you lack that experience, begin with the position of systems security analyst, associate.

Using the format noted in the example that follows, determine what
skills you need, the estimated completion date (ECD), and the actual completion date (ACD). Note that the format identifies the professional and
technical education and experience needed.

Technical skills are related to information systems, such as programming, system security software installation and maintenance, access control, and any other function that falls under the InfoSec category (use the
categories noted for CISSPs, if you feel uncomfortable in defining the skills
at a more finite level).

Professional experience and education are related to the general,
professional education and experience needed as an ISSO, such as
project management, time management, and how to develop and present
briefings. College, university, and technical schools should also be noted
under Education.

Sample Outline for a Systems Security Analyst

Education Needs

Professional   *ECD/ACD*
1. Time Management
2. Project Management
3.
4.
5.

Technical   *ECD/ACD*
1. C++
2. TCP/IP
3. UNIX
4.
5.

Experience Needs

Professional   *ECD/ACD*
1. Project Leading
2.
3.
Technical   *ECD/ACD*
1. Programming
2.
3.

Remember, your personal career development plan is dynamic and needs constant updating and self-reevaluation. December is a good time to assess your year's successes and failures. It also is a good time to begin preparation for next year's challenges and opportunities. So, be sure to update your plan and keep it current.

By establishing the plan, using the information provided in this chapter, you can save time by focusing on specific goals and accomplishments. As they say, "How do you eat an elephant? A bite at a time."

SUMMARY

1. ISSO career development planning helps ensure the ISSO an opportunity for a successful career.
2. Career development planning requires an understanding of ISSO positions and the education, training, experience, and certification needed.
3. Education and training can come from many sources, such as trade journals, universities, conferences, and technical schools.
4. Experience can be gained by volunteering to assist others in InfoSec and information systems functions.
5. The information provided in this chapter not only will help you on your ISSO career path but, eventually, can be used for helping members of your staff on their paths to career development.

5

How to Market Yourself as an ISSO

CHAPTER OBJECTIVE

The objective of this chapter is to provide the person seeking to be an ISSO or a current ISSO a unique approach to assist in obtaining the desired ISSO position and developing a personal ISSO portfolio for use during the job interview.

INTERVIEWING FOR THE ISSO POSITION

Congratulations, your resume finally made it through the filtering process and you are being asked to appear for an interview. You probably will find very talented ISSO professionals competing against you for the position. As with most job interviews these days, you are likely to be subjected to a series of interviews with members of the human resources department, information systems organization, auditors, and security personnel. Do not be nervous, but this interview is what will put you back on the road to ISSO job hunting or offer you the challenges of the new ISSO position. So, you must be prepared.

Many books on the market tell you how to interview for a position. They offer advice on everything from how to dress to how to answer the "mother of all interview questions"—*What are your salary expectations?* It is not the purpose of this book to help you answer those common interview questions. We assume that you will have read those books, prepared, and practiced for the upcoming interview. The purpose of this chapter is to show you how you can separate yourself from your ISSO competition.

You probably already interviewed more times than you care to admit. In all those interviews, like your peers, you walked in wearing dark, conservative business attire, neatly groomed, and prepared to answer any question thrown at you. The question is, *What separated you from your competitors?* What would make the interviewers remember you and choose you above the rest?

You probably answered most questions the most politically correct way. Question: *What is your major weakness?* Answer: *My major weakness is that I have very little patience for those who don't live up to their commitments. When someone agrees to complete a project by a specific date, I expect that date to be met unless the project leader comes to me in advance of the deadline and explains the reason why that date cannot be met. I believe in a team effort, each of us vital members of the team, working together to provide the service and support needed to assist the company in meeting its goals.*

Will that answer to the question be considered a weakness or a strength by the interviewers? Probably a strength, but that is how the game is played.

Most of us have been there, done that, and still did not get the position. Why? Maybe because such answers "float" in the interview room air. They hang there mingling with those of the other candidates before and after us. The only real lasting evidence of the interview is what was written down by the interviewers, the impressions you, the prospective ISSO, left in their minds. Many of the interviewers are "screeners," human resource people who have no clue as to what InfoSec is all about. They are there because we work as teams today. We operate by consensus. So, getting selected is much more difficult.

You need one thing that will have a lasting impression on the interviewers. One thing that will show them you have the talent, the *applied* education (that is, education you learned in college and actually can use in the business world), the experience *and* the game plan. You already have done it. You have been successful in building an InfoSec program before and you will be successful again. You can prove that you can do it because you have your ISSO portfolio.

The next question the reader may ask is, *What the heck is my ISSO portfolio?* You probably have seen movies where the models show up at the photography or movie studio and present their folders, containing photographs of themselves in various poses. No, your photo probably will not help you get the ISSO position, but think about the idea behind these folders. The models brought to their interviews physical evidence, in the form of photographs, that *proved* they were the best candidates for the position. You must develop your own portfolio and leave the interviewers *proof* that you have been there, done that. You are the best candidate for the position. It is all there in the portfolio.

You should begin building your ISSO portfolio as soon as you begin your first ISSO job—or before. It should contain a table of contents and identified sections that include letters of reference, letters of appreciation, copies of award certificates, project plans, metric charts you use for measuring the success of your InfoSec programs, and probably most important, your InfoSec philosophy and InfoSec plan outline that you will implement as soon as you are hired.

The InfoSec Plan may be the most important document in your portfolio and should be the first page after your table of contents. All the other documents are just proof that what you plan to do, you have done before. If you never have been an ISSO, you can build your InfoSec plan and InfoSec portfolio from the information provided in this book. Build it for TCI.

The next question that may arise is, *If I never worked there, how do I know what I should do if I get hired?* Again, do some research. Remember, if you really want this job, you have to at least work as hard to get it as you will once you do get it.

Your first stop should be the Internet. Find out about the company. Some information which you should know is

1.   When was it started?
2.   What are its products?
3.   How is the company stock doing?
4.   Where are its offices located?

Find out the answers to the "who? how? where? why? what? when?" of the company. Also, stop by the company and pick up an application, any company brochures available, including benefits pamphlets and the like.

Study the information, complete the application, and place it in your portfolio. After all, if the company decides to hire you, you will have to fill out one anyway. Go into the interview knowing as much, if not more, about the company as the people interviewing you. This is invaluable, especially as you interview for more senior level positions. These interviews undoubtedly will include the members of executive management. Your ability to talk about the company in business terms with an understanding of it undoubtedly will impress these managers and indicate that you are business-oriented.

All your answers to the interviewer's questions should be directed to something in your portfolio. For example, if you are asked how you would deal with downsizing in your department and what impact that would have on your ability to adequately protect the company's information and its related systems, you should be able to direct the questioner to a process chart, a metric, something that indicates that you have done it before and have a business-oriented approach to dealing with the issue. If you have not done it before, write down how you could, how you would, perform these functions, such as assess the affect on the InfoSec program.

The portfolio can work for any new ISSO in any company. The following sample portfolio outline can be used as a guide by a new or experienced ISSO. In this case, it is the ISSO applying for the TCI ISSO position. It is up to you to fill in the details. Many of the ideas of what to put in your InfoSec portfolio will be found in this book.

Note that the prospective ISSO applying for the TCI position has done the research necessary to tailor an InfoSec program to TCI. The beauty of building this type of portfolio is that it seems specific and, yet, it is generic.

SAMPLE ISSO PORTFOLIO OUTLINE

Table of Contents

I.   Introduction
II.   The Position and TCI Values
III.   Strategic Objectives
IV.   Tactical Objectives
V.   Transition Plan and the Future
VI.   Why I Am the Right ISSO for TCI
VII.   Examples of a Proven ISSO Record That Will Meet
        TCI's Expectations and Needs

I. Introduction

Purpose

I want to tell you about me, my InfoSec-related education and experience, and how I can establish and lead an InfoSec program for TCI based on a cost-effective philosophy for providing InfoSec services and support to our internal and external customers. (Note: A good technique to use during the interview is to use *we* and *our* in your discussions. This will help get the interviewers to look at you as a TCI team member. Approach it as if you already worked at TCI and you were in a TCI meeting discussing InfoSec issues.)

Objective

My objectives are to convince you that I am the most qualified and best person for the position of ISSO for TCI and to explain how we can establish a business-oriented InfoSec program for TCI.

II. The Position and TCI Values

The following is how I view the position of TCI ISSO:

Customers

1.   We must meet our customers' reasonable expectations;
2.   We must show by example that we are the best in the industry in meeting any of their InfoSec needs.

Within TCI

1.   As the TCI ISSO, I will establish and manage an InfoSec program that supports business needs and requirements;
2.   As the TCI ISSO, I will strive for an InfoSec program that adds value to TCI's products and services.

TCI Suppliers

1.   We will advise suppliers so they can develop high-quality InfoSec products that meet TCI's needs at a reasonable price;
2.   To do this, we will assist them in understanding our InfoSec needs;
3.   We will direct them to offer us only products that can be integrated into the TCI InfoSec program, cost effectively, with minimal maintenance.

Quality

1.   We will establish and manage an InfoSec program that provides high-quality service and support to its internal and external customers;
2.   We will provide that quality service and support with least impact on cost and schedules.

Integrity

1.   As the ISSO, I will follow the rules, both the spirit and the intent;
2.   I will always be honest;
3.   I will be ethical at all times.

Leadership

1.   I will lead by example;
2.   I will help others follow that example.

III. Strategic Objective

We will build a comprehensive InfoSec environment that supports TCI's business needs at the lowest cost and least impact on schedules with the minimum risk to TCI's business, information, and systems.

IV. Tactical Objectives

1.   Define detailed milestones for TCI's comprehensive InfoSec environment, which is identified as the TCI strategic objective;
2.   Describe the current TCI InfoSec environment;
3.   Identify the difference between 1 and 2;
4.   Establish a master project and schedule to meet the strategic, tactical, and annual objectives as integral parts of TCI's business plans.

V. Transition Plan and the Future

The plan will begin as soon as I come onboard. In week 1 at TCI, I expect to:

1.   Begin transition meetings with management to discuss expectations, goals, objectives, and budget;
2.   Begin my familiarization with TCI processes and how systems are being used at TCI by all key departments;
3.   Begin a review of TCI policies and procedures that relate to InfoSec;
4.   Establish appointments to meet with applicable department heads to discuss their ideas related to InfoSec and how it may help or hinder their operations.

In Week 2, I will:

1.   Hold one-on-one meetings with each department head;
2.   Hold in-depth interviews with peers in InfoSec-related organizations;
3.   Begin scoping the InfoSec level of effort required.

Week 3 will focus on:

1.   Coordination of personnel and organizational issues with the HR staff;
2.   Coordination of InfoSec-related problems, issues, and constraints.

During Week 4, I will:

1.   Finalize InfoSec plans, including the strategic, tactical, and annual plans;
2.   Begin recruitment and hiring, as applicable;
3.   Continue coordination meetings with applicable peers and executive management.

For the rest of the first year, I plan to:

1.   Develop, implement, and manage InfoSec projects;
2.   Develop InfoSec metrics and manage the InfoSec program;

3. Continue working on InfoSec issues with the TCI InfoSec team;
4. Continue evaluating potential InfoSec cost reductions based on cost-risk assessments;
5. Near year-end, analyze successes and failures, validate goals and objectives, and plan projects for the next year;
6. Continue to evaluate various InfoSec program processes and make changes where necessary to keep it fresh, active, and viable.

From the beginning of next year through the year 2000, I will:

1. Continue to assess and refine the first year goals;
2. Increase and enhance the skills of our InfoSec organization and staff members;
3. Ensure that TCI's InfoSec program becomes an integrated, value-added program.

VI. Why I Am the Right ISSO for the TCI Position

(This section includes the highlights of your resume. A copy of the resume should also be inserted here. Remember, do not use a boilerplate resume. Tailor the resume for the TCI job based on the "advertised" TCI job description.)

1. My bachelor's degree in InfoSec shows that I have the educational background to understand the academic and technical aspects of the profession.
2. My MBA shows that I have the business and management background to understand TCI from a business perspective.
3. I have experience in supporting and providing services and support to similar customers.
4. Attached is proof that I enjoy the trust and confidence of other professional ISSOs, in both government agencies and business. (Refer the interviewers to your letters of appreciation.)
5. I have detailed knowledge of all InfoSec-related federal and state laws and regulations. (Note: The ISSO should identify all federal and state laws that apply.)
6. I have a detailed knowledge of information systems, their threats, areas of vulnerability, and associated risk.
7. My references show that I enjoyed the trust and confidence of corporate management wherever I have been employed.
8. A proven InfoSec plan already is prepared, tailored for TCI, and ready for implementation.
9. Attached is my previous experience in coordinating related activities with the local district attorney, FBI, local police, and Secret Service.

10.   I am experienced in InfoSec, management, and leadership; for example, working on government standards, active on committees, working groups, and so forth. (Refer interviewers to your attachments "proving" your statement.)

VII. Examples of a Proven ISSO Record That Will Meet TCI's Expectations and Needs

This section should be used to demonstrate examples of your work, broken down into the following subsections:

1.   Functional costs averages (in this subsection, list all the information related to past budget, tracking, etc.);
2.   Project management (in this subsection, list samples of project management tracking, e.g. Gantt charts).
3.   Metrics management (in this subsection, list the metrics you have developed or would use to manage InfoSec functions).

SUMMARY

1.   Prior to being interviewed for TCI's ISSO position, learn all you can about TCI.
2.   Read books about how to prepare and dress for interviews.
3.   Prepare answers for the typical questions you may be asked, and practice the interview process so your answers come across as natural and not memorized, rehearsed answers.
4.   Develop an ISSO portfolio to be used during the interview.
5.   During the interview, refer the interviewers to the portfolio.
6.   During the interview, use "we" and "our" as if you already worked at TCI.

6

The ISSO's Position, Duties, and Responsibilities

CHAPTER OBJECTIVE

The objective of this chapter is to define the role that the ISSO will play in a corporation or government agency. In this case, it is the role of the ISSO for TCI. The duties and responsibilities of an ISSO vary depending on the place of employment. However, in this case, we assume the ISSO has the *perfect* position.

THE ISSO POSITION

The ISSO position is extremely important, as that person is the in-house consultant on InfoSec matters. The ISSO also represents TCI to the *outside world* on InfoSec matters. If you are chosen as the new ISSO, you should have determined the history of that position. When was it established? Why? What is expected of the ISSO? What happened to the last one? (You want to know so you can understand the political environment in which you will be working.) Those questions should have been asked—and answered—during the interview process. If not, get them answered now.

As you begin your new job as the TCI ISSO, you must clearly determine what is expected of you. What are your responsibilities and duties? For what are you accountable? Again, this information should have been asked during your interview for two reasons: (1) so you know what you are getting into by accepting the ISSO position with TCI; and (2) so you can better prepare for the position with a more detailed InfoSec program prior to your first day at work.

You need a detailed plan prior to beginning your employment at TCI because you will be behind from the moment you walk into TCI. That is because putting together an InfoSec program from the start is a tremendous project. The ISSO has to determine what is important and requires protection; what is being protected and in what manner; if a staff is needed; if so, how many people with what qualifications for what positions; what tasks are to be performed; and the list goes on. On top of that is learning TCI, its culture, normal corporate policies, and procedures—all the learning that comes with joining a company.

As the new TCI ISSO, you cannot afford to waste any time in your 12–14 hour, time-consuming days. You must understand and learn your new environment, the key players, and the issues that must be addressed first.

The TCI ISSO eventually must get into a proactive mode to be successful; that is, identify problems and solutions *before* they come to the attention of management. This will happen when the problem adversely affects costs or schedules. And, remember, adverse impacts on costs and schedules run contrary to the InfoSec program goals, objectives, and the like.

When an ISSO is in the position of constantly *putting out fires,* the proactive InfoSec battle is lost. If that battle is lost, the results produce adverse impacts on costs and schedules. Therefore, the goal of a cost-effective InfoSec program probably could not be attained.

WHAT IS EXPECTED OF YOU?

You have been told that you are expected to establish and manage an InfoSec program that works and is no burden on TCI. You are told to establish the program you believe is necessary to get the job done. You have the full support of management because it has come to realize how important the information and systems are to TCI in maintaining its competitive advantage in the marketplace. This *honeymoon* will last about six months. So, take advantage of it. To do so, you need to hit the ground running and then pick up speed.

Based on the "blank management check" and your prior experience (or, for the inexperienced ISSO, the information gained reading this book), you have evaluated the TCI environment and decided that your overall goal at TCI is to *administer an innovative InfoSec program that minimizes security risks with least impact on costs and schedules, while meeting all of TCI's and customers' reasonable expectations.*

If that is what is expected of you, then that is your primary goal. Everything you do as the TCI ISSO should be directed toward meeting that goal. This includes

- Writing the InfoSec strategic plan,
- Writing the InfoSec tactical plan,
- Writing the InfoSec annual plan,
- Determining how the InfoSec department is organized,
- Determining what functions are to be established,
- Determining the process flow of those functions.

THE TCI ISSO'S RESPONSIBILITIES

As TCI's ISSO, you have certain duties and responsibilities. These include the following:

1. *Managing people,* which includes:
   Building a reputation for professional integrity,
   Maintaining excellent business relationships,
   Dealing with changes,
   Communicating with others,
   Influencing people in a positive way,
   Building a teamwork environment,
   Developing the potential of people through performance management,
   such as directing and helping InfoSec staff members to be results oriented.
2. *Managing the business of InfoSec,* which includes:
   A commitment to results,
   Focusing on customers and suppliers,
   Making decisions and taking responsibility for them,
   Developing and managing resource allocations,
   Planning and organizing,
   Being a problem solver,
   Thinking strategically,
   Using sound business judgment,
3. *Managing InfoSec processes,* which includes:
   Project planning and implementation,
   Maintaining high quality standards in everything,
   Maintaining a systems perspective,
   Maintaining current job knowledge.

GOALS AND OBJECTIVES

Remember that your primary goal is to administer an innovative InfoSec program that minimizes security risks at the least impact on costs and schedules, while meeting all of TCI's and customers' reasonable expectations. You must have as your objectives at least the following:

1. Enhance the quality, efficiency, and effectiveness of the InfoSec organization,

2. Identify potential problem areas and strive to mitigate the problems before TCI management or customers identify them,
3. Enhance the company's ability to attract customers because of its ability to efficiently and effectively protect information,
4. Establish the InfoSec organization as the InfoSec leader in the widget industry.

LEADERSHIP POSITION

As the ISSO, you will be a leader. In that position, it is extremely important that you understand what a leader is and how a leader is to act. The definition of *leadership* found in numerous dictionaries and management books focuses on the position or guidance of a leader, a person who leads, directing, commanding, or guiding a group or activity and the ability to lead.

As a *leader,* you must set the example, create and foster an information protection conscience within the company.

As a *corporate leader,* you must communicate the company's community involvement, eliminate unnecessary expenses, inspire corporate pride, and find ways to increase profitability.

As a *team leader,* you must encourage teamwork, communicate clear direction, create an InfoSec environment conducive to working as a team, and treat others as peers and team members not as competitors.

As a *personal leader,* you must improve your leadership skills, accept and learn from constructive criticism, take responsibility for decisions, make decisions in a timely manner, and demonstrate self-confidence.

PROVIDING INFOSEC SERVICE AND SUPPORT

As the ISSO and leader of an InfoSec service and support organization, you must be tuned especially to the needs, wants, and desires of your customers, both those within the company, your internal customers, and those outside the company, your external customers, usually the company's customers.

To provide service and support to your external customers, you must

1. Identify their information protection needs,
2. Meet their reasonable expectations,
3. Show by example that you can meet their expectations,
4. Treat customer satisfaction as priority number 1,
5. Encourage feedback and listen,
6. Understand their needs and expectations,
7. Treat customer requirements as an important part of the job,
8. Establish measures to assure customer satisfaction,
9. Provide honest feedback to customers.

To provide service and support to your internal customers, you must

1. Support their business needs,
2. Add value to their services,
3. Minimize the impact of security on current processes,
4. Follow the same guidelines as for external customers.

The TCI ISSO also will deal with suppliers of InfoSec products. These suppliers are valuable allies, because they can explain to you the many new InfoSec problems being discovered, how their products mitigate those problems, and generally keep you up-to-date on the latest news within the ISSO profession.

In dealing with suppliers of InfoSec-related products, you should[1]

1. Advise them of your needs and what types of products can help you;
2. Assist them in understanding your requirements and the products you want from them, including what modifications they must make to the products before you are willing to purchase them;
3. Direct them in the support and assistance they are to provide you;
4. Respect them as team members;
5. Value their contributions;
6. Require high-quality products and high standards of performance from them;
7. Recognize their needs, too.

USE TEAM CONCEPTS

It is important that the TCI ISSO understand that TCI's InfoSec program is a company program. To be successful, the ISSO cannot operate independently but as a team leader with a team of others who also have a vested interest in the protection of the company's information and information systems.

Remember that if the InfoSec functions are divided among two or more organizations (e.g., asset protection and physical security of hardware under the security department), there naturally will be a tendency for less communication and coordination. The ISSO must be sensitive to this division of functions and ensure that even more communication and coordination occurs between all the departments concerned.

The program must be sold to the management and staff of TCI. If it is presented as a "law that must be obeyed" or else, then it will be doomed to failure. The ISSO will never have enough staff members to monitor everyone

---

[1] If you recall, we discussed cost-effective ways to keep current in the ISO profession. This is another way of doing it.

all the time, and that is what will be needed. As soon as the ISSO's back is turned, the employees will do things the way they want to. Everyone must do it the right InfoSec way because they know it is the best way and in their own interests, as well as in the interest of TCI.

In TCI, as in many companies today, success can be achieved only through continuous interdepartmental communication and cooperation, with specialists from various departments formed into integrated project teams to solve company problems. The ISSO should keep in mind that teamwork and success go together in today's corporation.

VISION, MISSION, AND QUALITY STATEMENTS

Many of today's corporations have developed vision, mission, and quality statements using a hierarchical process. The statements, if used, should link all levels in the management and organizational chain. The statements of the lower levels should be written and used to support the upper levels and vice versa.

The following examples can be used by the ISSO to develop such statements, if they are necessary. And as you can already guess, they are required at TCI.

Vision Statements

In many of today's businesses, management develops a vision statement. The vision statement usually is a short paragraph that attempts to set the strategic goal, objective, or direction of the company.

TCI has a vision statement and requires all organizations to have statements based on the TCI corporate statements.

A vision statement is *a short statement that is clear, concise, and understandable by the employees; connected to the firm's ethics, values, and behaviors; states where TCI wants to be (in the long term); and sets the tone and direction for TCI.*

TCI Vision

The company will design, produce, and sell a high-quality widget, thereby expanding its market share while continuing to improve processes to meet customers' expectations.

TCI's Information Technology Department Vision Statement[2]

In partnership with our customers, we will provide a competitive advantage for the TCI widget by continuous maximization of available technol-

---

[2] If you recall, the ISSO reports to the director of the information technology department.

ogy to enhance productivity and cost-effectively support increased production of TCI widgets.

InfoSec Vision Statement

InfoSec will provide the most efficient and effective InfoSec program for TCI, one that adds value to TCI products and services as a recognized leader in the widget industry.

Mission Statements

Mission statements are declarations of the purpose of a business or government agency.

TCI's Mission Statement

TCI's mission is to maintain its competitive advantage in the market place by providing widgets to its customers when they want them, where they want them, and at a fair price.

TCI's Information Technology Department Mission Statement

The mission of TCI's information technology department is to provide low-cost, productivity-enhanced, technology-based services that will assist TCI in maintaining its competitive advantage in the marketplace.

InfoSec Mission Statement

InfoSec will administer an innovative program that minimizes security risks at the least impact on costs and schedule, while meeting all of the company's and customers' InfoSec requirements.

Quality

Quality is what adds value to a company's products and services. It is what your internal and external customers expect from you.

TCI's Quality Statement

TCI will provide high-quality widgets to its customers with zero defects by building it right the first time.

TCI's Information Technology Department Quality Statement

The department will provide high-quality information systems' support and services that will enhance the productivity opportunities of the TCI workforce.

InfoSec Quality Statement

The program consistently will provide high-quality InfoSec professional services and support that meet the customers' requirements and reasonable expectations, in concert with good business practices and company guidelines.[3]

INFORMATION SYSTEMS PROTECTION PRINCIPLES

An ISSO's duties and responsibilities are many and sometimes quite complex and conflicting. However, as the TCI ISSO, you must never lose sight of the three basic InfoSec principles: access control, individual accountability, and audit trails. This triad of InfoSec must be incorporated into the TCI InfoSec program. For just as a three-legged milking stool requires three strong and level legs, the InfoSec program requires these three strong principles. Without them, the InfoSec program will topple just like a two-legged milking stool.

PROJECT AND RISK MANAGEMENT PROCESSES

Two basic processes that are an integral part of an InfoSec program are project management and risk management.

Project Management

As the InfoSec manager and leader for TCI you also will provide oversight on InfoSec-related projects being worked by members of your staff.

The criteria for a project is as follows. Formal projects, along with project management charts, will be initiated where improvements or other changes will be accomplished and where that effort has an objective, beginning and ending date, and will take longer than 30 days to complete.

If the project will be accomplished in less than 30 days, a formal project management process is not needed. The rationale for this is that projects of short duration are not worth the effort (costs in terms of hours to complete the project plan, charts, etc.) of such a formal process.

---

[3] You will find that the same themes of service, support, cost-effectiveness, customer expectations, and so on continuously runs through this book. We hope that the constant reinforcement will cause you to continuously think of these themes when establishing and managing an InfoSec program.

Risk Management

To be cost effective, the ISSO must apply risk management concepts and identify:

1. Threats to the information and information systems of TCI,
2. Areas of vulnerability (information systems' weaknesses),
3. Risks,
4. Countermeasures to mitigate against those risks in a cost-effective way.

INFOSEC ORGANIZATIONAL RESPONSIBILITIES

As the TCI ISSO, you will manage and lead an InfoSec organization. You will be responsible for developing, implementing, maintaining, and administering a company-wide InfoSec program.

Suppose you have evaluated the TCI environment and found that a centralized program is required to cost-effectively *jump-start* the InfoSec program and its associated processes. Your evaluation of what is needed led you to consider the following InfoSec-related functions for development:[4]

1. Management of all functions and work routinely accomplished during the course of conducting the organization's business in accordance with TCI's policies and procedures;
2. System access administration and controls, which include the direct use and control of the systems' access software, monitoring its use, and identifying access violations;
3. Access violation analyses to identify patterns and trends that may indicate an increased risk to the systems or information;
4. Computer crime and abuse inquiries where there are indications of intent to damage, destroy, modify, or release to unauthorized people information of value to the company (note that this function was coordinated and agreed to by the Director of Security as long as his investigative organization manager was kept apprised of the inquiries and copies of all reports sent to that manager);
5. Disaster recovery and contingency planning, which includes directing the development and coordination of a companywide program to mitigate the possibility of loss of systems and information and assure their rapid recovery in the event of an emergency or disaster;

---

[4] As previously mentioned, TCI is the ideal company for an ISSO and, therefore, we are developing an ideal InfoSec program and organization.

6.   An awareness program established and administered to all system users to make them aware of the information systems protection policies and procedures that must be followed to adequately protect systems and information;
7.   Evaluation of the systems' hardware, firmware, and software for any possible impact on the security systems and information;
8.   Where applicable, risk assessments conducted and the results reported to management for risk management decisions;
9.   Systems' compliance inspections, tests, and evaluations to ensure that all users and systems are in compliance with TCI's InfoSec policies and procedures.

THE TCI ISSO'S FORMAL DUTIES AND RESPONSIBILITIES

Based on the preceding and in concert with the executive management of TCI, the ISSO developed and received approval for formally establishing the following charter of TCI ISSO responsibilities.

Summary of the Purpose of the TCI ISSO Position

The TCI ISSO will develop, implement, maintain, and administer an overall, TCI-wide InfoSec program, which includes all plans, policies, procedures, assessments, and authorizations necessary to ensure the protection of customer, subcontractor, and TCI information from compromise, destruction, and unauthorized manipulation while processed, stored, or transmitted by TCI's information systems.

Accountability

•   Identify all government, customer, and TCI InfoSec requirements necessary for the protection of all information processed, stored, or transmitted by TCI's information systems; interpret those requirements; and develop, implement, and administer TCI plans, policies, and procedures necessary to ensure compliance.
•   Evaluate all hardware, firmware, and software for any possible impact on the security of the information systems; direct and ensure their modification if requirements are not met; and authorize their purchase and use within TCI and applicable subcontractor locations.
•   Establish and administer the technical security countermeasures program to support TCI requirements.

- Establish and administer a security tests and evaluations program to ensure that all the information systems of TCI and applicable subcontractors are operating in accordance with their contracts.
- Identify, evaluate, and authorize for use all information systems and other hardware within TCI and at applicable subcontractor locations to ensure compliance with "red/black" engineering[5] where proprietary and other sensitive information is processed.
- Direct the use of and monitor TCI's information systems access control software systems, analyze all systems' security infractions and violations, and report the results to management and human resources personnel for review and appropriate action.
- Identify information systems business practices and security violations and infractions, conduct inquiries, assess potential damage, direct and monitor TCI management's corrective action, and implement or recommend corrective and preventive action.
- Establish and direct a TCI-wide telecommunications security working group.
- Develop, implement, and administer a risk assessment program; provide analyses to management; modify TCI and subcontractor requirements accordingly to ensure a lowest-cost InfoSec program.
- Establish and administer an InfoSec awareness program for all TCI information systems users, including customers and subcontractor users, to ensure they are cognizant of information systems threats and the security policies and procedures necessary for the protection of information systems.
- Direct and coordinate a TCI-wide information systems disaster recovery and contingency planning program to assure the rapid recovery of information systems in the event of an emergency or disaster.
- Direct the development, acquisition, implementation, and administration of InfoSec software systems.
- Represent TCI on all InfoSec matters with customers, government agencies, suppliers, and other outside entities.
- Provide advice, guidance, and assistance to TCI management relative to InfoSec matters.
- Perform common management responsibilities in accordance with TCI's management policies and procedures.

---

[5] For TCI, red/black engineering means the methods used to separate those data lines that require special protection because of the sensitivity of the information flowing through them from those lines that require no enhanced protection. A main concern with such lines running together is the chance that emanations will transfer between the lines, thus exposing "protected" information to compromise.

SUMMARY[6]

1. The ISSO position is a leadership position within a company.
2. The recently hired ISSO must know what is expected of the company's new ISSO and should have a clear understanding of those expectations before taking the position.
3. The three primary responsibilities of an ISSO are managing people, managing the InfoSec business, and managing the InfoSec processes.
4. The ISSO must set forth clear goals and objectives.
5. The ISSO must be a company leader, team leader, and personal leader.
6. The ISSO must provide InfoSec service and support using concepts of teamwork.
7. The ISSO should develop vision, mission, and quality statements as guides to developing a successful InfoSec program.
8. The ISSO should strive to administer an InfoSec program where all the major InfoSec functions are under the responsibility of the ISSO.

---

[6]Much of the information in this chapter provides details that could be used in the ISSOs portfolio, as noted in the portfolio sample outline presented in the previous chapter.

7

The InfoSec Strategic, Tactical, and Annual Plans

CHAPTER OBJECTIVE

The objective of this chapter is to establish the plans for the InfoSec organization that provide the subsets of the TCI strategic, tactical, and annual plans. These plans will set the direction for TCI's InfoSec program while integrating the plans into TCI's plans, thus indicating that the InfoSec program is an integral part of TCI.

TCI'S INFOSEC STRATEGIC PLAN

To be successful, the TCI ISSO must have an InfoSec Strategic Plan (ISP). That plan should be integrated, or at least compatible, with TCI's Strategic Business Plan (seven-year plan), which sets the long-term direction, goals, and objectives for the InfoSec program.

As stated in Chapter 3, TCIs Strategic Business Plan sets forth the following information:

1. The expected annual earnings for the next seven years;
2. The market-share percentage goals on an annual basis;
3. The future process modernization projects based on expected technology changes of faster, cheaper, and more powerful computers, telecommunications systems, and robotics;

4.   TCI expansion goals;
5.   TCI's acquisition of some current subcontractor and competitive companies.

The TCI ISP is the basic document on which to base the TCI InfoSec program with a goal of building a comprehensive InfoSec environment at the lowest cost and least impact on the company.

When developing the ISP, the ISSO must ensure that the following basic InfoSec principles are included, either specifically or in principle (because it is part of the InfoSec strategy):

1.   Minimize the probability of security vulnerability,
2.   Minimize the damage if any vulnerability is exploited,
3.   Provide a method to recover efficiently and effectively from the damage.

The TCI Strategic Business Plan also called for a mature InfoSec program (within the next seven years) that could (1) protect TCI's information while allowing access to its networks by its international and national customers, subcontractors, and suppliers and (2) support the integration of new hardware, software, networks, and the like while maintaining the required level of InfoSec with no impact on schedules or costs.

The InfoSec Strategic Plan Objective

The objectives of the ISP are to

1.   Minimize risk to systems and information,
2.   Minimize impact on costs,
3.   Minimize impact on schedules,
4.   Assist in meeting contractual requirements,
5.   Assist in meeting noncontractual requirements,
6.   Build a comprehensive systems security environment,
7.   Maintain flexibility to respond to changing needs,
8.   Support multiple customers information protection needs,
9.   Incorporate new technologies as soon as needed,
10.   Assist in attracting new customers,
11.   Maximize the use of available resources.

ISP and Teamwork: Concepts, Communication, and Coordination

A successful InfoSec program also must deal with the office politics of the TCI environment. A key element, which was stated earlier in this book, is to remember that the information and information systems belong to TCI and not the ISSO. Therefore, cooperation and coordination are a must.

Many functional organizations have an interest in the ISP and other InfoSec-related plans; therefore, the plans should be discussed with other team members such as the auditors, security personnel, human resources personnel, and company legal staff. The ISP also should be discussed with key members of the user community and TCI managers and their input requested. After all, what you do affects what they do. This is a great way to establish communication and interaction, which will lead to a better plan, with broad-based support.

The input and understanding by these people of what the TCI ISSO is trying to accomplish will assist in ensuring TCI-wide support for the InfoSec plans. Only with the help of others can the ISSOs TCI's InfoSec program succeed.

ISP Planning Considerations

The ISP planning considerations also must include

1. Good business practices,
2. High-quality management,
3. Innovative ideas,
4. An InfoSec vision statement,
5. An InfoSec mission statement,
6. An InfoSec quality statement,
7. Channels of open communication with others, such as the auditors, systems personnel, security personnel, users, and management.

All these factors must be considered when developing an InfoSec strategy and documenting that strategy in the TCI ISP.

The TCI process flow of plans begins with the TCI Strategic Business Plan through the TCI Annual Business Plan. Each plan's goals and objectives must be able to support the other, top down and bottom up (Figure 7.1). Once this process is understood, the next step is to map the TCI ISP into the TCI Strategic Business Plan goals and objectives.

Mapping TCI's InfoSec Strategic Plan to the TCI Strategic Business Plan

TCI's strategy identified the annual earnings for the next seven years as well as market-share percentage goals. This clearly underscores the need for an InfoSec program that will be cost-effective.

As previously mentioned, InfoSec is a "parasite" on the profits of TCI if it cannot be shown to be a value-added (needed to support the bottom line) function. Therefore, the InfoSec strategy must be efficient (cheap) and effective (good). If this can be accomplished, then the InfoSec program will be in a position to support the TCI's strategy relative to earnings and market share.

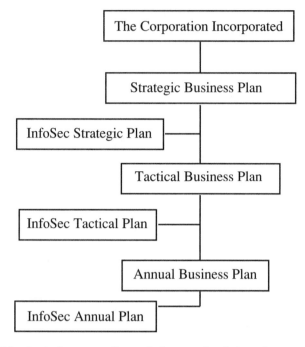

Figure 7.1 The logical process flow of plans and InfoSec plan's integration into the TCI flow.

Mapping these points (Figures 7.1 and 7.2) can help the ISSO visualize a strategy prior to documenting that strategy in the InfoSec strategic plan. Such mapping also will assist the ISSO in focusing on the strategies that support the TCI strategies.[1]

Writing the InfoSec Strategic Plan

Writing the ISP will be much easier after the mapping is completed. Once that is accomplished, the ISSO will write the ISP following the standard TCI format for plan writing.

The TCI format was determined to be as follows:

1. Executive Summary,
2. Table of Contents,
3. Introduction,

---

[1]For those readers who are inclined to argue the technical definitions of terms, remember that the definition of terms varies between corporations and those used here may not fit neatly into the definitions used by your corporation or government agency. However, do not lose sight of the process being discussed; that is the important aspect of this chapter.

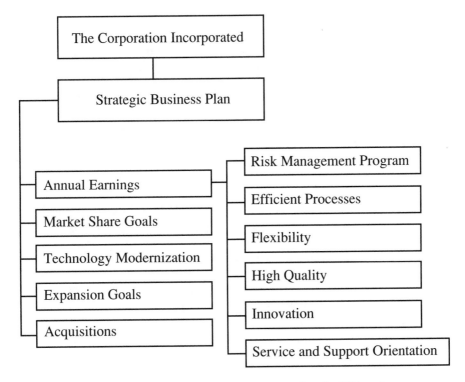

Figure 7.2 A sample mapping of a TCI strategic goal to the ISP goals.

4. Vision Statement,
5. Mission Statement,
6. Quality Statement,
7. InfoSec Strategic Goals,
8. Explanation of How the InfoSec Strategies Support the TCI Strategies,
9. Mapping Charts,
10. Conclusion.

TCI'S INFOSEC TACTICAL PLAN

A tactical plan is a short-range (three-year) plan that supports the TCI ISP goals and objectives. The InfoSec tactical plan (ITP) should

1. Identify and define, in more detail, the vision of a comprehensive InfoSec environment, as stated in the ISP;
2. Identify and define the current TCI InfoSec environment;
3. Identify the process to be used to determine the differences between the two.

Once this is accomplished, the ISSO can identify projects to progress from the current TCI InfoSec environment to where it should be, as stated in the ISP. In the ITP, it is also important to keep in mind TCI's business directions, its customers' directions, and the direction of technology. Once that is established, individual projects can be identified and implemented, beginning with the InfoSec annual plan (IAP).

The TCI Tactical Business Plan stated that "In addition, the program is expected to be able to integrate new hardware, software, networks, and the like with *minimal* impact on schedules or costs." Therefore, it will be necessary to establish a project with the objective of developing a process to accomplish that goal.

The ISSO also must consider that the TCI InfoSec program must contain processes to reevaluate the mechanisms used to protect information so that it is protected for only the period required. Therefore, a project must be established to accomplish that goal.

The TCI Tactical Business Plan also called for the *completion* of an InfoSec program that could protect TCI's information while allowing access to its networks by its international and national customers, subcontractors, and suppliers. Therefore, another project must be developed to accomplish this goal (Figure 7.3).

Writing the InfoSec Tactical Plan

Writing the ITP should be somewhat easier based on the experience gained in mapping the goals for the ISP, ITP, and writing the ISP. Once that is accomplished, the ISSO will write the ITP, following the standard TCI format for plan writing.

The TCI format was determined to be as follows:

1.   Executive Summary,
2.   Table of Contents,
3.   Introduction,
4.   Specification of the InfoSec Strategic Goals,
5.   Explanation of How the InfoSec Tactics Support the ISP,
6.   Explanation of How the InfoSec Tactics Support TCI Tactics,
7.   Mapping Charts,
8.   Conclusion.

TCI'S INFOSEC ANNUAL PLAN

The ISSO must develop an InfoSec annual plan (IAP) to support the TCI ISP and ITP. The plan must include the goals, objectives, and projects that will support the goals and objectives of TCI's Annual Business Plan.

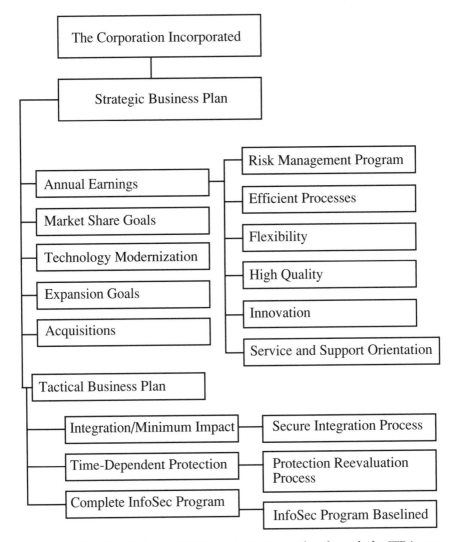

Figure 7.3 Mapping from the TCI Strategic Business Plan through the ITP in support of the TCI Tactical Business Plan.

TCI's InfoSec annual plan is to be used to identify and implement projects to accomplish the goals and objectives stated in the ISP and ITP.

Remember, the InfoSec program requires the following:

1. Project management techniques,
2. Gantt charts (schedule),
3. An identified beginning date for each project,

4. An identified ending date for each project,
5. An objective for each project,
6. Cost tracking and budget,
7. Identification of the responsible project leader.

InfoSec Annual Plan Projects

The initial and major project of the TCI ISSO's first IAP is to identify the current TCI InfoSec environment. To understand the current TCI environment, culture, and philosophy, the following projects are to be established:

1. Project Title: TCI InfoSec Organization

    Project Leader: ISSO
    Objective: Establish an InfoSec Organization
    Starting Date: January 1, 1998
    Ending Date: July 1, 1998

2. Project Title: InfoSec Policies and Procedures Review

    Project Leader: ISSO
    Objective: Identify and review all InfoSec-related TCI documentation and establish a process to ensure applicability and currency
    Starting Date: February 1, 1998
    Ending Date: April 1, 1998

3. Project Title: InfoSec Team

    Project Leader: ISSO
    Objective: Establish a TCI InfoSec working group to assist in establishing and supporting an InfoSec program
    Starting Date: January 1, 1998
    Ending Date: February 1, 1998

4. Project Title: TCI Proprietary Process Protection

    Project Leader: InfoSec Organization Systems Security Engineer
    Objective: Identify, assess, and protect TCI proprietary processes
    Starting Date: April 15, 1998
    Ending Date: September 1, 1998

5.   Project Title: InfoSec Organizational Functions

    Project Leader: ISSO

    Objective: Identify and establish InfoSec organizational functions and their associated processes and work instructions

    Starting Date: January 15, 1998

    Ending Date: July 1, 1998

6.   Project Title: InfoSec Support to IT Changes

    Project Leader: InfoSec Organization Systems Security Engineer

    Objective: Establish a process to provide service and support to integrate InfoSec as changes are made in the IT environment

    Starting Date: March 15, 1998

    Ending Date: October 1, 1998

Mapping the TCI IAP to the TCI Annual Business Plan

As previously shown, the TCI InfoSec annual plan easily can be mapped to the TCI Annual Business Plan. However, in this case, the TCI annual plan objectives were not indicated nor used to map the IAP, except as shown in Figure 7.4.[2]

WRITING THE INFOSEC ANNUAL PLAN

As noted already, the plans must follow the TCI format. The TCI IAP is no exception, and the following format is required:

1.   Executive Summary,
2.   Table of Contents,
3.   Introduction,
4.   Specification of the InfoSec Annual Goals,
5.   Specification of the InfoSec Projects,
6.   Explanation of How the InfoSec Projects Support the TCI's Annual Plan Goals,
7.   Mapping Charts,
8.   Conclusion.

---

[2] By now, you should understand this process and be able to use this mapping method.

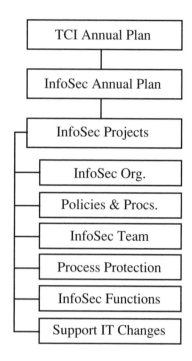

Figure 7.4   Mapping IAP projects to the TCI Annual Business Plan.

MAPPING ISP, ITP, AND IAP TO PROJECTS USING A MATRIX

Another approach to mapping employs a matrix. This method can be used in a number of ways and at various levels, such as mapping the TCI Strategic Business Plan to the ISP. In Figure 7.5, some mapping areas intentionally are left blank to show how easy it is to identify those items that map to others and, more important, those that do not. This method can identify "holes" in your plans that must be addressed.

SUMMARY

1.   The TCI InfoSec strategic, tactical, and annual plans must be mapped and integrated into the TCI Strategic, Tactical, and Annual Business Plans.
2.   The InfoSec plans must incorporate the InfoSec vision, mission, and quality statements, their philosophies and concepts.
3.   The InfoSec plans must identify the strategies, goals, objectives, and projects that support each other and the TCI plans.

Projects	ISP	ITP	IAP
InfoSec Org.	X	X	X
Policies & Procs.			X
InfoSec Team			X
Process Protection	X		X
InfoSec Functions		X	X
Support IT Changes		X	X

Figure 7.5 Matrix mapping, which also can show the relationship—or a lack of one—between items.

4. By mapping the goals of the TCI plans with those of the InfoSec plans, the required information fusion can be determined and shown graphically.
5. Mapping will make it easier for the ISSO to write the applicable InfoSec plans.
6. The InfoSec annual plan generally consists of the projects that form the building blocks of the InfoSec program following the strategies and tactics of the ISP and ITP.

8

Establishing an InfoSec Organization

CHAPTER OBJECTIVE

The objective of this chapter is to describe and discuss the establishment and management of the organization chartered with the responsibility to lead the InfoSec effort for TCI, including structuring and describing the organization and the job descriptions of the personnel to be hired to fill the positions within the InfoSec organization.

**THE ISSO'S THOUGHT PROCESS
IN ESTABLISHING THE INFOSEC ORGANIZATION**

The TCI ISSO now must begin the arduous task of establishing an InfoSec program and organization. In doing so, the ISSO must understand the limits of authority, the amount of budget available, and the impact of establishing an InfoSec program on TCI—the culture change.

The ISSO also must determine how to find qualified people who can build and maintain a cost-effective InfoSec program. The staff must be able to develop into an InfoSec team, where everyone acts and is treated as a professional, a group of InfoSec professionals who are very talented and yet leave their egos at the door when they come to work (not an easy task for very talented people).

The ISSO must consider that building an *empire* and a massive bureaucratic organization not only will give the wrong impression to TCI management but it will be costly. Furthermore, the ISSO must build an efficient and effective InfoSec organization, as required by TCI and as stated in the numerous plans. After all, that was one of the implied conditions of employment.

Building a bureaucracy leads to cumbersome processes, which leads to slow decision cycles, which causes InfoSec to have an adverse impact on costs and schedules for TCI, which leads to an InfoSec program that does not provide the services and support needed by TCI. This snowballing effect, once started, will be difficult to stop. And, if stopped, it requires twice as long to rebuild the service and support reputation of the ISSO and the InfoSec program.

In developing the InfoSec organization, the ISSO also must bear in mind all that has been discussed with TCI management and what was promised, including:

1. TCI's history, business, and the competitive environment;
2. TCI and InfoSec's mission, vision, and quality statements;
3. TCI and InfoSec plans;
4. The need to develop an InfoSec program as quickly as possible, for the work will not wait until the ISSO is fully prepared.

DETERMINING THE NEED FOR INFOSEC SUBORDINATE ORGANIZATIONS

The ISSO must determine whether or not subordinate organizations are needed. If so, a functional work breakdown structure must be developed to determine how many subordinate organizations are needed and what functions should be integrated into what subordinate organizations.

The ISSO reviews the InfoSec charter previously agreed to by the ISSO and executive management. This charter includes the following InfoSec functions:

1. Requirements, policies, procedures, and plans;
2. Hardware, firmware, and software InfoSec evaluations;
3. Technical security countermeasures;
4. InfoSec tests and evaluations;
5. Information system processing approvals;
6. Access control;
7. Noncompliance inquiries;
8. Telecommunications security;
9. Risk management;
10. Awareness and training;
11. Disaster recovery and contingency planning.

The ISSO analyzed the plans, functions, number of systems, and number of users, then determined that two subordinate organizations would be needed to provide the minimum InfoSec professional services and support. Actually, the ISSO thought of dividing the functions into three organizations but decided that, not only would that give the wrong impression to others in TCI (always remember perceptions and how things may appear when building an InfoSec program and organization), the organizations would provide another level of administrative overhead burden, which would not be cost effective. Therefore, the ISSO reasoned that the two subordinate organizations would suffice for now and the organizations could be reevaluated at the end of the first year's operation.

The ISSO decided to brief the director of IT (The Boss) on the plan. The director thought it was reasonable but wondered how the ISSO would handle the off-site location.

As with any good plan, nothing ever runs completely as expected. Being an honest and straightforward ISSO, the only logical comeback was, "Huh?" The director went on to explain that the company's small, off-site location manufactures subassemblies of the widgets and ships them to the main plant. The off-site plant is located approximately 125 miles from the main plant.

The ISSO asked the director how other organizations handled the off-site plant. The director explained that they have smaller satellite offices to provide the service and support needed at that location. The ISSO determined that, before deciding on the need for a satellite office, the problem should be evaluated further. The ISSO explained to the director that the evaluation would be conducted within a week and a decision made at that time.

The ISSO subsequently determined that, to provide high-quality services and support to the off-site plant, a small InfoSec organization should be established at that time. This decision was based on several considerations:

1. Conversations with managers of other organizations who had satellite offices at the off-site location relative to how they handled the problem,
2. Conversations with managers of other organizations who did *not* have satellite offices at the off-site location as to how they handled the service and support requirements,
3. Analysis of the off-site location's information systems configuration and processing,
4. Information flow processes,
5. The InfoSec needs of that location.

Based on the analysis, the ISSO determined that an InfoSec satellite office indeed was necessary, but some functions could be supported from the main plant, such as risk management, InfoSec policy development, plans, and requirements.

The ISSO informed the Director of IT of the decision and the basis for it, emphasizing the decision's cost-effectiveness. The Director agreed, based on the business logic shown by the ISSO and what the Director sensed as the ISSO's strong commitment to InfoSec using a lowest-cost/minimum risk approach.

DEVELOPING THE INFOSEC
ORGANIZATION STRUCTURE

Based on these analyses, the ISSO established the InfoSec organization—at least on paper (Figure 8.1). The ISSO found that establishing the InfoSec organization to date was the easy part. Now came the bureaucracy of coordinating and gaining approval of the InfoSec organization from the designated organizations in the company (for example, Organizational Planning, Human Resources, Facilities) as well as completing their forms and other organizations' forms.[1]

As a word of caution to the ISSO, some *service and support* organizations are more interested in proper completion of the administrative bureaucracy than helping their internal customers. Just grin and bear it.

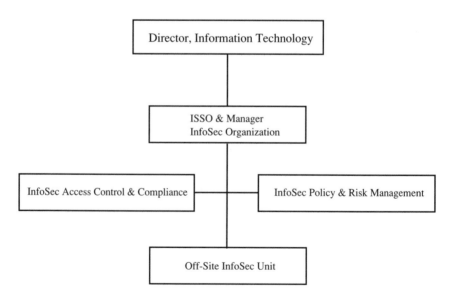

Figure 8.1   A sample InfoSec high-level organization structure.

---

[1] Because each corporation has a somewhat different *forms bureaucracy,* no attempt will be made here to complete any forms. Those readers who have to make any changes in an organization can appreciate the maze the ISSO now must go through.

You cannot change the process, except over time and now is not the time. Getting the InfoSec program and organization off the ground takes priority. Concentrate on that priority.

DEVELOPING THE INFOSEC SUBORDINATE ORGANIZATIONS

The ISSO determined that the subordinate organizations also must have charters that identify the InfoSec functions to be performed by the staff of that organization. The ISSO further determined that to recruit managers for the subordinate organization was premature. What was needed first were professional InfoSec personnel who could begin the actual InfoSec work. The ISSO would manage all the organizations until such time as the workload and cost-effectiveness considerations determined that a subordinate manager or managers were needed.

Based on the work to be performed and the analyses discussed previously, the ISSO developed the charters for three subordinate organizations.

RESPONSIBILITIES OF INFOSEC SUBORDINATE ORGANIZATIONS

InfoSec Access Control and Compliance Subordinate Organization

The ISSO is the acting manager of the InfoSec Access Control and Compliance (IACC) subordinate organization.

Position Summary

The IACC is to provide the management and direction and conduct analyses required to protect information processed on TCI information systems from unauthorized access, disclosure, misuse, modification, manipulation, or destruction as well as implement and maintain appropriate information and information systems access controls, conduct noncompliance inquiries, and maintain violations tracking systems[2] (see Figure 8.2).

Detailed accountability includes

1. Implementation, administration, and maintenance of user access control systems by providing controls, processes, and procedures to

---

[2] The ISSO decided that InfoSec's highest priority was the TCI systems and information at the company's facilities. The sticky problem of dealing with non-TCI InfoSec issues, such as subcontractors and customers, would have to wait. The ISSO reasoned that if TCI had a successful, professional program, it would be easier to gain the cooperation of the outside corporations.

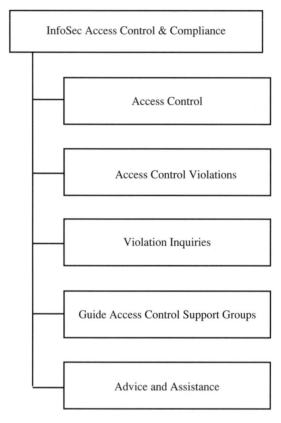

Figure 8.2   An InfoSec subordinate organization and its primary functions.

prevent the unauthorized access, modification, disclosure, misuse, manipulation, or destruction of TCI information.

2.   Monitoring user access control systems to provide for the identification, inquiry, and reporting of access control violations. Analysis of system access controls violations' data and trends to determine potential systems' security weaknesses and report to management.

3.   Conducting inquiries into InfoSec violations and incidents and related InfoSec business practices, TCI policies, and procedures. Identification of the exposures or compromises created and recommendations to management for corrective and preventive actions.

4.   Direction, monitoring, and guidance of the InfoSec activities of TCI's access controls support groups and systems to ensure adequate implementation of access control systems in meeting InfoSec requirements.

5.   Provision of advice and assistance in the interpretation and implementation of InfoSec policies and procedures, contractual InfoSec requirements, and related documents.

InfoSec Policy and Risk Management

The ISSO is the acting manager of the InfoSec policy and risk management subordinate organization.

Position Summary

The InfoSec Policy and Risk Management organization is to provide the management; direction; and develop, implement, and maintain InfoSec policies and procedures; user awareness of risks, disaster recovery; and contingency planning; InfoSec system life-cycle processes, InfoSec tests and evaluations; risk management; InfoSec technical security; related programs to protect TCI systems and information (Figure 8.3).

Detailed accountability includes:

1. Identification of all InfoSec requirements needed and development of TCI policies and procedures necessary to assure conformance to those requirements.
2. Evaluation of all hardware, software, and firmware to ensure conformance to InfoSec policies and procedures, recommendation of modifications when not in conformance, and approval when in conformance.
3. Establishment and administration of an InfoSec test and evaluation program to ensure compliance with systems' security documentation and applicable InfoSec requirements.

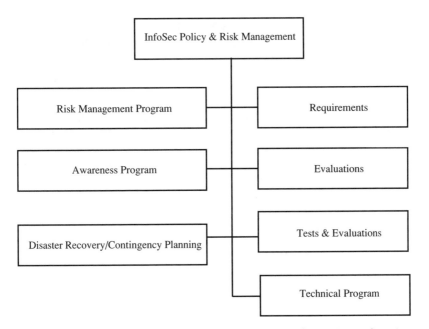

Figure 8.3 Another InfoSec subordinate organization and its primary functions.

4.   Establishment, implementation, and maintenance of an InfoSec technical program to identify all electronic threats and mitigate against those threats in a cost-effective manner.
5.   Establishment and maintenance of an InfoSec awareness program to ensure TCI management and users are cognizant of InfoSec policies, procedures, and requirements for the protection of systems and information and their related threats.
6.   Development, implementation, and administration of a risk management program to identify and assess threats, vulnerabilities, and risks associated with the information for which TCI has responsibility and recommendation of cost-effective modifications to the InfoSec program, systems, and processes.
7.   Establishment and maintenance of a disaster recovery and contingency planning program that will protect InfoSec, TCI information, and systems against losses and assure the successful recovery of the information and systems with a minimal impact on TCI.

Off-Site InfoSec Organization

The ISSO is the acting manager of the off-site InfoSec subordinate organization. However, the ISSO has determined that it also will be necessary to appoint a person supervisor to manage the day-to-day operations of the off-site InfoSec program. The supervisor has authority to make decisions related to that activity, with several exceptions. The supervisor can not counsel the InfoSec staff, evaluate their performance (except to provide input to the InfoSec manager), make new InfoSec policy, or manage budgets.

Position Summary

The supervisor is to implement, maintain, and administer an InfoSec program for TCI resources at the off-site location and take the action necessary to ensure compliance with the InfoSec program requirements, policies, and procedures to protect TCI information from compromise, destruction, and unauthorized manipulation[3] (Figure 8.4). Detailed accountability includes:

1.   Implementation and administration of TCI plans, policies, and procedures necessary to ensure compliance with the stated TCI InfoSec requirements for the protection of all information processed, stored, and transmitted on TCI information systems.

---

[3] Because of its off-site location, this position requires InfoSec functions be performed that are similar or the same as those of most functions noted for the entire InfoSec organization.

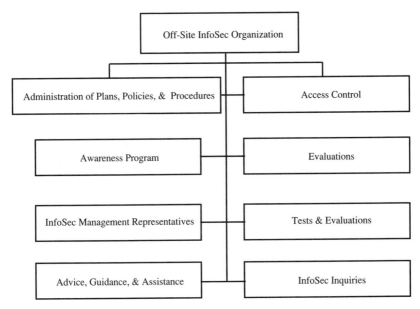

Figure 8.4   The off-site InfoSec subordinate organization and its primary functions.

2.   Administration of an InfoSec test and evaluation program to ensure that all TCI information systems are operated in accordance with appropriate InfoSec requirements and contract specifications.

3.   Administration and monitoring of the local use of TCI information systems access control software systems, analysis of all infractions and violations, documentation and reports of the results of questionable user activity for InfoSec inquiries.

4.   Identification of information systems' business practice irregularities and security violations and infractions, conducting detailed inquiries, assessment of potential damage, monitoring TCI management's corrective actions, and recommendation of preventive measures to preclude recurrences.

5.   Administration of an InfoSec awareness program for all TCI managers and users of TCI information systems to ensure they are cognizant of information systems, threats and are aware of the InfoSec policies and procedures necessary for the protection of information and information systems.

6.   Representation of the InfoSec manager in all applicable TCI InfoSec matters as they apply to personnel, resources, and operations at the off-site location.

7.   Provision of advice, guidance, and assistance to management, system users, and systems' custodians relative to InfoSec matters.

8.   Performance of other functions as designated or delegated by the InfoSec manager.

INFOSEC JOB DESCRIPTIONS

After establishing and gaining final approval for the InfoSec organization, while trying to begin establishing a formal, centralized InfoSec program, the ISSO determined it was time to begin hiring InfoSec professionals. However, before that could be accomplished and in accordance with TCI Organizational Development and Human Resources requirements, an InfoSec job family first had to be established. After all, TCI, being a high-tech, modern corporation, requires that employees be assigned to career families to support their career development program as directed by the Human Resources department. Unfortunately, InfoSec had never been a formal part of TCI and, therefore, no current job families seem to meet the needs of the InfoSec functions.

The ISSO and the Human Resources person discussed the matter and agreed that the ISSO would write the InfoSec functional job family descriptions. The ISSO is told that the descriptions must be generic enough and flexible enough to support several InfoSec job functions within each level of the job family. The Human Resources person advised the ISSO that this is necessary to ensure the flexibility needed for recruiting, hiring, and the subsequent career development of the InfoSec professionals. Also, it would streamline the process and ensure that the number of InfoSec job family positions' descriptions could be kept to a minimum, thus decreasing bureaucracy and paperwork.

At the conclusion of the meeting, the Human Resources person provided the ISSO with the job descriptions for the security, auditor, and information technology job families, along with several forms that must be completed when submitting the InfoSec job family descriptions, as well as forms to be used for documenting each job family description by grade level.

Armed with the challenges of this new onslaught of bureaucratic paper and bidding adieu to the Human Resources person, the ISSO headed back to the office to begin writing TCI's InfoSec job family as sample descriptions (while wondering when there will be time to do *real* InfoSec work).

After reviewing the provided job descriptions and reading the paperwork needed to *make this all happen*, the ISSO wrote and provided the Human Resources person the InfoSec job family functional descriptions. After several iterations and compromises, and approvals through a chain of organizational staffs, the job family was approved.

INFOSEC JOB FAMILY
FUNCTIONAL DESCRIPTIONS[4]

The following detailed InfoSec job family functional descriptions were developed and approved by the applicable TCI departments.

---

[4] These detailed job descriptions are based on the summary job descriptions found in Chapter 4.

Systems Security Administrator

Position Summary

The Systems Security Administrator is to provide all technical administrative support for the InfoSec organization, including filing, typing reports, word processing, and developing related spreadsheets, databases, and text and graphic presentations.

Qualifications

The qualifications include a high school diploma and one year of security administration or two years of clerical experience plus the ability to type at least 60 words per minute.

System Security Analyst, Associate

Position Summary

The Associate Systems Security Analyst is to assist and support InfoSec staff in ensuring all applicable TCI InfoSec requirements are met.

Duties and Responsibilities

1.   Support the implementation and administration of InfoSec software systems.
2.   Provide advice, guidance, and assistance to system users relative to InfoSec matters.
3.   Identify current InfoSec functional processes and assist in the development of automated tools to support those functions.
4.   Assist in the analysis of manual InfoSec functions and provide input to recommendations and reports of the analyses to InfoSec management.
5.   Maintain, modify, and enhance automated InfoSec functional systems of InfoSec tests and evaluations, risk assessments, software and hardware evaluations, access control, and other related systems.
6.   Collect, compile, and generate InfoSec functional informational reports and briefing packages for presentation to customers and management.
7.   Perform other functions as assigned by InfoSec management.

The position requires being assigned to perform duties in one or more of the following areas:

• *Access Control.* Maintain basic user access control systems by providing processes and procedures to prevent unauthorized access or the destruction of information.

- *Access Control: Technical Access Control Software.* Assist access controls support groups and systems by providing software tools and guidance to ensure adequate implementation of access control systems in meeting InfoSec requirements.
- *Access Control: Violations Analysis.* Monitor the use of TCI access control software systems, identify all systems InfoSec infractions and violations, and document and report the results of questionable user and system activity for InfoSec inquiries.
- *InfoSec Tests and Evaluation: InfoSec System Documentation.* Perform InfoSec tests and evaluations on stand-alone (nonnetworked) systems to ensure the systems are processing in accordance with applicable InfoSec-approved procedures.

Qualifications

This position normally requires a bachelor's degree in an InfoSec-related profession.

System Security Analyst

Position Summary

The Systems Security Analyst is to identify, schedule, administer, and perform assigned technical InfoSec analyses functions to ensure all applicable requirements are met.

Duties and Responsibilities

1. Represent InfoSec to other organizations on select InfoSec-related matters.
2. Provide advice, guidance, and assistance to managers, system users, and system custodians relative to InfoSec matters.
3. Provide general advice and assistance in the interpretation of InfoSec requirements.
4. Identify all InfoSec requirements necessary for the protection of all information processed, stored, and transmitted by the information systems and develop and implement plans, policies, and procedures necessary to ensure compliance.
5. Identify current InfoSec functional processes and develop automated tools to support those functions.
6. Analyze manual InfoSec functions and provide recommendations and reports of the analyses to InfoSec management.
7. Maintain, modify, and enhance automated InfoSec functional systems of InfoSec tests and evaluations, risk assessments, soft-

ware and hardware evaluations, access control, and other related systems.

8. Collect, compile, and generate InfoSec functional informational reports and briefing packages for presentation to customers and management.

9. Perform other functions as assigned by InfoSec management.

The position requires being assigned to perform duties in the following areas:

- *Access Controls: Technical Access Control Software.* Administer and maintain user access control systems by providing controls, processes, and procedures to prevent the unauthorized access, modification, disclosure, misuse, manipulation, or destruction of TCI information.
- *Access Controls: Violations Analysis.* Administer and monitor the use of TCI access control software systems, analyze all systems InfoSec infractions and violations, and document and report the results of questionable user and system activity for InfoSec inquiries.
- *Noncompliance Inquiry:* Identify and analyze InfoSec business practice irregularities and InfoSec violations and infractions, conduct detailed inquiries, assess potential damage, monitor corrective action, and recommend cost-effective preventive measures to preclude recurrences.
- *Risk Assessment:* Perform limited risk assessments of InfoSec systems and processes; determine their threats, vulnerabilities, and risks; and recommend cost-effective risk mitigation solutions.
- *InfoSec Tests and Evaluation: InfoSec System Documentation.* Schedule and conduct InfoSec tests and evaluations on stand-alone (nonnetworked) systems to ensure the systems are processing in accordance with applicable InfoSec-approved procedures.

Qualifications

This position normally requires a bachelor's degree in an InfoSec-related profession and at least two years of practical experience.

System Security Analyst, Senior

Position Summary

The Senior Systems Analyst is to identify, evaluate, conduct, schedule, and lead technical InfoSec analyses functions to ensure all applicable TCI InfoSec requirements are met.

Duties and Responsibilities

1. Provide technical analysis of InfoSec requirements necessary for the protection of all information processed, stored, or transmitted by systems; interpret those requirements; and translate, implement, and administer division plans, policies, and procedures necessary to ensure compliance.
2. Represent InfoSec on security matters with other entities, as assigned.
3. Provide advice, guidance, and assistance to senior management, systems' managers, system users, and custodians relative to InfoSec matters.
4. Perform other functions as assigned by InfoSec management.

The position requires being assigned to perform duties in the following areas:

*   *Access Control: Technical Access Control Software.* Implement, administer, and maintain systems' user access control systems through the use of controls, processes, and procedures to prevent their unauthorized access, modification, disclosure, misuse, manipulation, or destruction.
*   *Access Control: Violations Analysis.* Coordinate, administer, and monitor the use of systems' access control systems; analyze systems' security infractions and violations employing statistical and trend analyses and report the results.
*   *InfoSec Awareness:* Prepare, schedule, and present InfoSec awareness briefings to systems' managers, custodians, and users. Act as focal point for dissemination of InfoSec information through all forms of media.
*   *Disaster Recovery:* Coordinate and ensure compliance with system disaster recovery and contingency plans to assure the rapid recovery of the system in the event of an emergency or disaster.
*   *Hardware and Software InfoSec Evaluation:* Evaluate all hardware, firmware, and software for any possible impact on the InfoSec of the systems; monitor and ensure their modification if requirements are not met; and authorize their purchase and use within TCI.
*   *Noncompliance Inquiry:* Identify and conduct technical analyses of InfoSec business practices and violations and infractions; plan, coordinate, and conduct detailed inquiries; assess potential damage; and develop and implement corrective action plans.
*   *Risk Assessment.* Conduct limited InfoSec technical risk assessments and prepare reports of the results for presentation to management
*   *InfoSec Tests and Evaluations: InfoSec Documentation.* Schedule and conduct InfoSec tests and evaluations to ensure that all the applicable systems are operating in accordance with InfoSec requirements.

- *Technical Countermeasures.* Conduct technical surveys and determine necessary countermeasures related to physical information leakage and conduct sound attenuation tests to ensure information processing systems do not emanate information beyond TCI's zone of control.

Qualifications

This position normally requires a bachelor's degree in an InfoSec-related profession and four years of practical related experience.

System Security Analyst, Specialist

Position Summary

The Specialist Systems Security Analyst is a technical InfoSec advisor, the focal point and leader to ensure all InfoSec functions are meeting TCI requirements as well as developing and administering applicable programs.

Duties and Responsibilities

1. Act as technical advisor for InfoSec requirements necessary for the protection of all information processed, stored, or transmitted by systems; interpret those requirements; and translate, document, implement, and administer TCI InfoSec plans, policies, and procedures necessary to ensure compliance.
2. Represent InfoSec on security matters with other entities, as assigned.
3. Provide advice, guidance, and assistance to senior management, IT managers, system users, and system custodians relative to InfoSec matters.
4. Perform other functions, as assigned by InfoSec management.

The position requires being assigned to perform duties in a combination of the following areas:

- *Access Controls: Technical Access Control Software.* Implement, administer, and maintain systems' user access control systems through the use of controls, processes, and procedures to prevent their unauthorized access, modification, disclosure, misuse, manipulation, or destruction.
- *InfoSec Awareness.* Prepare, schedule, and present InfoSec awareness briefings to systems' managers, custodians, and users. Act as focal point for dissemination of InfoSec information through all forms of media.
- *Disaster Recovery.* Coordinate and ensure compliance with system disaster recovery and contingency plans to assure the rapid recovery of systems in the event of an emergency or disaster.

- *Hardware and Software InfoSec Evaluations.* Evaluate all hardware, firmware, and software for any possible impact on the InfoSec of the systems; monitor and ensure their modification if requirements are not met; and authorize their purchase and use within TCI.
- *Risk Assessment.* Conduct limited InfoSec technical risk assessments and prepare reports of the results for presentation to management.
- *InfoSec Tests and Evaluations: InfoSec Documentation.* Schedule and conduct InfoSec tests and evaluations to ensure that all the applicable systems are operating in accordance with InfoSec requirements.
- *Technical Countermeasures.* Conduct technical surveys and determine necessary countermeasures related to physical information leakage and conduct sound attenuation tests to ensure information processing systems do not emanate information beyond TCI's zone of control.

Qualifications

This position normally requires a bachelor's degree in an InfoSec-related profession and six years of InfoSec experience.

System Security Engineer

Position Summary

The System Security Engineer is a technical systems management consultant, the focal point and project leader for InfoSec functions and programs developed to ensure TCI requirements are met.

Duties and Responsibilities

1. Lead in the identification of government, customers, and TCI InfoSec requirements necessary for the protection of information processed, stored, or transmitted by TCI's systems; interpret those requirements; and develop, implement, and administer TCI InfoSec plans, policies, and procedures necessary to ensure compliance.
2. Represent the InfoSec office, when applicable, on InfoSec matters as well as serve as TCI's liaison with customers, government agencies, suppliers, and other outside entities.
3. Provide advice, guidance, and assistance to senior and executive management, TCI's subcontractors, and government entities relative to InfoSec matters.
4. Provide technical consultation, guidance, and assistance to management and systems' users and ensure the protection of InfoSec software systems by providing controls, processes, and procedures.

5. Establish, direct, coordinate, and maintain a disaster recovery and contingency program for TCI that will mitigate against systems and information losses and assure the successful recovery of the system and information with a minimal impact on TCI.

6. Lead in the technical evaluation and testing of hardware, firmware, and software for any possible impact on the security of the systems; direct and ensure their modification if requirements are not met; authorize their purchase and use within TCI; and approve them when in conformance.

7. Develop or direct the development of original techniques, procedures, and utilities for conducting InfoSec risk assessments; schedule and conduct InfoSec risk assessments; and report results to management.

8. Direct and lead others in conducting technical InfoSec countermeasure surveys to support InfoSec requirements and report findings.

9. Direct and administer InfoSec tests and evaluations programs to ensure that the applicable systems are operating in accordance with InfoSec requirements.

10. Provide technical consultation and assistance in identifying, evaluating, and documenting use of systems and other related equipment to ensure compliance with communications requirements.

11. Investigate methods and procedures related to the InfoSec aspects of microcomputers, local area networks, mainframes, and their associated connectivity and communications.

12. Identify and participate in evaluation of microcomputer and local area networks InfoSec implementations, including antivirus and disaster recovery and contingency planning functions.

13. Perform development and maintenance activities on InfoSec-related databases.

14. Recommend and obtain approval for procedural changes to effect InfoSec implementations with emphasis on the lowest cost and minimum risk.

15. Lead and direct InfoSec personnel in conducting systems InfoSec audits.

16. Participate in the development and promulgation of InfoSec information for general awareness.

17. Perform other functions as assigned by the InfoSec manager.

The position requires being assigned to perform duties in a combination of the following areas:

- *Supervisor, Project Leader.* Provide assistance, advice, guidance, and act as technical specialist relative to all InfoSec technical functions.

Qualifications

This position normally requires a bachelor's degree in an InfoSec-related profession and a minimum of ten years of InfoSec-related experience.

RECRUITING INFOSEC PROFESSIONALS

Once the InfoSec organizational structure and job family functional descriptions both have been approved, the ISSO can begin recruiting and hiring qualified InfoSec professionals.

Hold it, not so fast! The ISSO first must determine the following:

1. How many InfoSec professionals are needed?
2. What functions will they perform?
3. How many are needed in each function?
4. How many are needed in what pay code?
5. How many should be recruited for the off-site location?
6. Does the off-site location or main plant have the higher priority?

The ISSO must plan for the gradual hiring of personnel to meet the InfoSec needs based on a listing of functions by priority. Obviously, a mixture of personnel should be considered. One or two high-level personnel should be hired to begin establishing the basic InfoSec processes. Personnel who meet the qualifications of a System Security Engineer should be hired immediately. At least two should be hired. One would be the project leader to begin the process of establishing the formal functions of one of the InfoSec subordinate organizations while the other would do the same for the other InfoSec organization.

At the same time, the access control function positions should be filled, as they represent the key InfoSec mechanism of access control.

Functions such as risk management, noncompliance inquiry, and an awareness program can come later. The rationale used by the ISSO for this decision is that InfoSec policies have not been established, so there is nothing on which to base noncompliance inquiries or an awareness program. The next position to be filled after the two Systems Security Engineers and Access Control personnel is the Disaster Recovery and Contingency Planning Specialist.

The ISSO reasoned that, although access controls were being tightened up and analyzed, the engineers were beginning to build the process for each function, with much of the assistance for access control process development being done with the assistance of the Access Control Administrators. In the event of a disaster, the systems must be up and operational in as short a time period as possible. This is crucial to the well-being of TCI.

Unfortunately, the type of individual the ISSO would want to employ usually is not readily available. In addition, TCI's policy is to *promote from within* whenever possible. So, although a *more* qualified individual may be available from outside TCI, the ISSO may have to transfer a less qualified individual, currently employed within TCI, because that person meets the minimum requirements for the position, at least as interpreted by the Human Resources personnel.

The ISSO soon begins to realize that compromise and coordination are a *must* for even a slight chance of succeeding in building the TCI InfoSec program. Based on some soul searching and the political climate, the ISSO decides to find as many people as possible within TCI who are willing to transfer and meet the minimum requirements for an InfoSec position. The ISSO soon learns why the job descriptions approved through the Human Resources department include words such as *normally* and *equivalent.* The ISSO naively thought that those words would assist in bringing in InfoSec professionals, not that others also could use the position descriptions to *help* recruit personnel, some who just barely meet the minimum requirements.

For the ISSO who is quickly trying to build an InfoSec Program and InfoSec organization, the compromises on staff selection may help or hurt. In either case, it is important to quickly begin the hiring process.

Identifying In-House InfoSec Candidates

Those individuals within TCI organizations who have been providing access control in either a full- or part-time position for their department's local area networks (LAN) may be good access control candidates. The IT department also may be a place to recruit InfoSec candidates. The audit and security departments may provide more InfoSec candidates.

As a word of caution, most managers do not take kindly to recruiting their employees, as they will be shorthanded until they can find replacements. In addition, the ISSO should beware of individuals who the managers recommend. The manager may have been trying to find some way to get rid of these people for some time.

The ISSO has enough problems building an InfoSec program, establishing and managing an InfoSec organization, handling the day-to-day InfoSec problems, attending endless meetings, trying to hire a professional InfoSec staff, and having to transfer personnel who do not meet the ISSO's expectations to be saddled with a *difficult* employee recommended by another manager. A difficult employee could occupy the ISSO's time more than three other staff members combined. It seems that the IT department has a penchant for this, so beware of *Geeks bearing gifts.*

Identifying Outside InfoSec Candidates

Many sources can be used for recruiting talented InfoSec professionals, sources limited only by imagination and budget (especially budget).

Regardless of how or where you recruit, the recruitment must be coordinated with the Human Resources staff.

To recruit InfoSec personnel, the TCI controller must validate and approve (on another form, of course) that there is budget set aside for the InfoSec organization to hire staff.

Once that hurdle is cleared, Human Resources personnel must validate that you have completed the necessary form describing the position you want to hire for, the minimum qualifications, and the pay range for that position. Luckily, all the ISSO has to do basically is to transcribe the general position description onto the new Human Resources form used for recruiting candidates and advertising the positions.

Just when the ISSO thinks that the door is open to recruit InfoSec professionals, a member of the Human Resources department mentions how boring the Human Resources job is, that it would be nice to transfer to another, more interesting area, and that the InfoSec job seems to be very exciting. Experience? Well, of course, the person is proficient is *using* a computer. Another common problem is the manager or staff member who has a cousin just graduating from college who would be perfect for the InfoSec position.

The ISSO soon begins to realize that building and managing an outstanding, state-of-the-art InfoSec program staffed by talented InfoSec professionals may become more of a dream than a reality.

Once the ISSO is able to fend off these and similar charges, the recruitment effort within and outside TCI can start in earnest. Some ways to recruit InfoSec professionals are through:

1.   Advertise in trade journals, local newspapers, and the like;
2.   Hire a consulting firm to find the right people;
3.   Pass the word among colleagues;
4.   Ask InfoSec associations to *pass the word;*
5.   Use the Internet to advertise the position.

With a few InfoSec personnel on board, the ISSO can begin to work on the InfoSec Program, beginning with defining the processes and functions of the InfoSec organization.

SUMMARY

1.   Establishing an effective and efficient InfoSec organization and program requires a detailed analysis and integration of all the information that has been learned through the entire process of becoming an ISSO at TCI.
2.   Determining the need for InfoSec subordinate organizations requires detailed analysis of TCI's environment and an understanding of how

to successfully apply resource allocation techniques to the InfoSec functions.

3. Once the need for InfoSec subordinate organizations is determined, the ISSO must determine what functions go in what organizations.

4. Establishing a formal InfoSec organization and InfoSec job family requires cooperation with Human Resources personnel and others; patience and understanding are mandatory.

5. An ISSO who establishes a new organization for a corporation will be compelled to live within a less than ideal corporate world, where forms and bureaucracies rule the day. To survive, the ISSO must understand how to use those processes efficiently and effectively.

6. In most corporations, currently employed personnel who desire an InfoSec position and meet the minimum InfoSec requirements must be hired over an individual from the outside.

7. Recruiting qualified InfoSec professionals can be accomplished only through a widespread recruitment effort, using many marketing media, and successful advertisement sometimes is dependent on the recruitment budget available.

9

Determining and Establishing InfoSec Functions

CHAPTER OBJECTIVE

The objective of this chapter is to describe and discuss the major functions to be performed by the InfoSec organization and describe the flow processes that can be used to establish the baseline in performing the functions.

DETERMINING MAJOR INFOSEC FUNCTIONS

There are many InfoSec functions; however, at TCI, the functions identified in the ISSO's responsibilities charter (Chapter 6) were the main ones that identified the baseline for the InfoSec program. Therefore, these are the basic functions that should be established and description of a flow process developed regarding how the functions should be performed. The basic functions are[1]

1. Identification of requirements;
2. Establishment of InfoSec policy;
3. Establishment of InfoSec procedures;

---

[1] As mentioned in the preceding chapter, the ISSO decided to initially allocate resources and budget only to those functions internal to TCI. Customers and subcontractor issues would have to wait until the initial program was established and matured somewhat. Therefore, some of the functions noted, which are related to customers and subcontractors, are not identified and described here, as the ISSO believes such issues cannot be addressed for at least six months.

4. Establishment of an awareness program;
5. Establishment of access control systems;
6. Evaluation of all hardware, firmware, and software for any possible impact on the security of the information systems;
7. Establishment of a security test and evaluations program;
8. Management of noncompliance inquiries;
9. Management of risk;
10. Establishment of a disaster recovery and contingency planning program.

THE VALUE OF INFORMATION

Before addressing the InfoSec functions the ISSO realized that, to provide an effective InfoSec program with the least impact on costs and schedules, it is important to establish a process to determine the value of information. The ISSO's reasoning is that no information should be protected any more than is necessary. The rationale used by the ISSO is as follows.

The value of information is time dependent. In other words, information has value for only a certain period of time. Information relative to a new, unique TCI widget must be highly protected, including the electronic drawings, diagrams, processes, and so forth. However, once the new widget is announced to the public, complete with photographs of the widget, selling price, and the like, much of the protected information no longer needs protection.

Information that once required protection to maintain the secrecy of this new widget no longer needs that protection. This will save money for TCI, because, as was stated numerous times throughout this book, security costs are a *parasite on the profits* of TCI. Those costs must be reduced or eliminated as soon as possible. The task of the ISSO and staff members is to continuously look for methods to accomplish this objective.

Determining the value of TCI's information is a very important task, but one done very seldom with any systematic, logical approach by a company or government agency. However, the ISSO believed that, to provide the program TCI required, this task should be undertaken.

The consequences of not properly classifying the TCI information could lead to overprotection, which is costly, or underprotection, which is risky and could lead to the loss of that information, thus profits. (In the case of classified government information, it could adversely affect national security.)

To determine the value of information, the ISSO must first understand what is meant by *information* and what is meant by *value*. The ISSO must properly categorize and classify the information, through knowing the guidelines set forth by government agencies or businesses for determining the value and protection requirements of that information. In addition, how the ISSO perceives the information and its value is crucial to classifying[2] it.

If the information has value, it must be protected and protection is expensive. One should protect only information that requires protection; only in the manner necessary, based on the value of that information; and only for the period required.

Who Determines the Value of Information?

One might ask, "Does all the information of a company or government agency have value?" If the ISSO were asked that question, what would be the response? The next question would be, "What information has no value?" Is it information that the receiver of the information determines has no value? What if the originator of the information says it has value? Who determines if information has value? These are questions that the ISSO must ask—and answer—before trying to establish a process to set a value on any information. As you read through this material, think about the information where you work, how it is protected, why it is protected, and so on.

The value of the information may be determined by the holder of the information. Each person places a value on the information in his or her possession. Information necessary to successfully complete someone's work is very valuable to that person; however, it may have no value to anyone else. For example, to an accountant, the accounts payable records may be very important and without them the accountant could not do his or her job. However, for the person manufacturing the company's product, the information has little or no value. Ordinarily, the originator determines the value of the information, and that person categorizes or classifies the information, usually in accordance with the established guidelines.

Three Basic Categories of Information

Although there are no standard categories of information, most people agree that information logically can be placed into three categories: personal, private information; national security (both classified and unclassified) information; and business information.

The value of *personal, private information* is an individual matter but also a matter for the government and businesses. Persons may want to keep private such information as their age, weight, address, cellular phone number, salary, and likes and dislikes. Many countries have laws that protect

---

[2] In the context used here, the term *classify* has nothing to do with its use as related to national security information, such as Confidential, Secret, and Top Secret.

information under some type of "privacy act." In businesses and government agencies, it is a matter of policy to safeguard certain information about an employee such as age, address, and salary. Although personal to the individual, others may require that information; but with access to that information comes an obligation to protect it because it is considered to have value.

National security classified information includes information that must be safeguarded by all in the interest of national security. It is mentioned here briefly because the process used to place a value on that information goes through more stringent analyses than for personal, private information or business information.

National security classified information is generally divided into three basic categories:

1. Confidential: loss of this information can cause damage to national security;
2. Secret: loss of this information can cause serious damage to national security;
3. Top Secret: loss of this information can cause grave damage to national security.

Other national security information is not classified, like that in these categories, but requires some lesser degree of control and protection because it has value, although less value. Such information includes

1. Information For Official Use Only,
2. Unclassified But Sensitive Information,
3. Unclassified Information.

Business information also requires protection based on its value. This information sometimes is categorized as

1. Company Confidential,
2. Company Internal Use Only,
3. Company Private,
4. Company Sensitive,
5. Company Proprietary,
6. Company Trade Secret.

The number of categories used will vary with each company; however, the fewer categories, the fewer problems in classifying information and also, possibly, fewer problems in the granularity of protection required. Again, the cost must be considered. The TCI ISSO has found that the categories Private, Internal Use Only, and Proprietary would meet the needs of the TCI

InfoSec program. This company information must be protected because it has value to the company. The degree of protection required also depends on the value of the information during a specific period of time.

Types of Valued Information

Generally, the types of information of value to the business and requiring protection are all forms of financial, scientific, technical, economic, or engineering information, including but not limited to data, plans, tools, mechanisms, compounds, formulas, designs, prototypes, processes, procedures, programs, codes, and commercial strategies, whether tangible or intangible and whether stored, compiled, or memorialized physically, electronically, graphically, photographically, or in writing. Examples of information requiring protection may include research, proposals, plans, manufacturing processes, pricing determinations, and product information.

Determining Information Value

Based on an understanding of information, its value, and some practical and philosophical thoughts on the topic as stated already, the ISSO must have some sense of what must be considered when determining the value of information.

When determining the value of information, the ISSO must assess what it cost to produce that information. Also to be considered is the cost in terms of damages caused to the company if it were to be released outside protected channels. Additional consideration must be given to the cost of maintaining and protecting that information. How these processes are combined determines the value of the information. Again, do not forget to factor in the time element.

Two basic assumptions should be considered in determining the value of information: (1) All information costs some type of resource(s) to produce, such as money, hours, use of equipment; and (2) not all information can cause damage if released outside protected channels. If the information cost something to produce (and all information does cost to produce) and no damage is done if released outside protected channels, then why protect it?

The time factor is a key element in determining the value of information and cannot be overemphasized. Here is an example of information that is not time dependent—or is it? A company picnic is to take place on May 22, 1996. What is the value of the information before, on, or after that date? Does the information have value? To whom? When?

If you're looking forward to the company's annual picnic, as was your family, the information as to when and where it was to take place had some value to you. Supposedly, you found out about it the day after it happened. Your family was disappointed, mad at you for not knowing, and you felt bad. To the company, the information had no value. However, not receiving that information caused you to be disgruntled and you blamed the company for your latest family fight. Your anger affected your productivity for a week.

This is a simple illustration, but it indicates the value of information depending on who has or does not have that information, as well as the time element. It also shows that what is thought to be information not worth a second thought may have repercussions costing more than the value of the information.

As another example, a secret, revolutionary widget was being built to compete in a very competitive market, to enter the marketplace on January 1, 1997. What is the value of that information on January 2, 1997? Again, to stress the point, one must consider the cost to produce the information and the damage done if that information were released.

If the information was expensive to produce and could cause damage if released, it must be protected. If it cost something to produce but could not cause damage if released, then why protect it? At the same time, be sensitive to dissemination. Information, to have value, to be useful, must get to the right people at the right time.

Company Internal Use Only Information Types and Examples

Company Internal Use Only information has these characteristics:

1.   Not generally known outside the company,
2.   Generally, difficult to determine through product inspection,
3.   Possibly useful to a competitor,
4.   Provides some business advantage over competitors.

Some examples are the company telephone book, company policies and procedures, and company organizational charts.

Company Private Information Types and Examples

Company Private information has these characteristics:

1.   Discloses technical or financial aspects of the company,
2.   Indicates the company's future direction,
3.   Describes portions of the company business,
4.   Provides a competitive edge,
5.   Identifies personal information about employees.

Some examples are personnel records, salary information, cost data, short-term marketing plans, and dates for unannounced events.

Company Sensitive Information Types and Examples

Company Sensitive information has these characteristics:

1. Provides a significant competitive advantage,
2. Could cause serious damage to the company,
3. Reveals long-term company direction.

Some examples are critical company technologies, critical engineering processes, and critical cost data.

Questions to Ask When Determining Value

When determining the value of your information, as a minimum, you should ask the following questions:

1. How much does it cost to produce?
2. How much does it cost to replace?
3. What would happen if I no longer had that information?
4. What would happen if my closest competitor had that information?
5. Is protection of the information required by law and, if so, what would happen if I did not protect it?

TCI INFOSEC FUNCTIONS
PROCESS DEVELOPMENT

The ISSO has learned that the development of a new InfoSec program requires the establishment of InfoSec functions for that program. Establishing a process for each function as the first task will assist in ensuring that the functions will begin in a logical, systematic way that will lead to a cost-effective InfoSec program.

Requirements Identification Function

The ISSO has determined that the drivers for any InfoSec program are the requirements for InfoSec, the reason for the InfoSec program. This *need* is further identified and defined and subsequently met by the establishment of the InfoSec functions. So, to begin the functions processes identification, it is important to understand the source of the requirements, the need. For TCI, it is as follows:

1. As stated by the TCI executive management, an InfoSec program is to protect TCI's competitive edge, which is based on information systems and the information that they store, process, and transmit;
2. Contractual requirements are specified in contracts with TCI customers, such as to protect customers' information;
3. Contractual requirements are specified in contracts with TCI subcontractors, such as to protect subcontractors' information;
4. Contractual requirements are specified in contracts with TCI vendors, such as to protect vendor information;
5. TCI further wants to protect its information and systems from unauthorized access by customers, subcontractors, and vendors;
6. Federal, state, and local laws applicable to TCI require, for example, protecting the privacy rights of individuals and corporations as they relate to the information stored, processed, and transmitted by TCI systems.

InfoSec Policy

Based on the requirements and InfoSec drivers just stated, the ISSO must develop an InfoSec policy, coordinate that policy with applicable department managers, and gain executive management approval for the TCI InfoSec policy.

The policy should be clear, concise, and written at a somewhat high level. It must conform to the TCI policy format, of course. The TCI InfoSec policy should not get bogged down in details at a systems identification level but set the InfoSec guidelines for the corporation.

The InfoSec policy should be distributed to all department managers, and that distribution should be done through a cover letter, signed by the CEO, President, or Chairman of the Board of Directors. The letter basically should state that the information is important to TCI's well-being and competitive edge and that the InfoSec policy documents provide the overall policy for protecting the competitive edge, which obligates all TCI employees to support the policy. The cover letter for TCI states:

To: All TCI Employees

Subject: Protecting TCI's Information and Competitive Edge

The advances in the technology of computers and telecommunications and our use of them has provided us with the opportunity to gain a competitive advantage. Therefore, aside from you, they are our most vital asset. They are a vital asset because they are used to run our business by transmitting, processing, and storing our vital information. All of us at TCI have derived great benefit from being able to access our systems and communicate across the corporation, as well as with our customers, suppliers, and subcontractors. At the same time, the TCI systems contain vital information that, if destroyed, modified, or disclosed to outsiders, would be harmful to the corporation and adversely affect our competitive edge.

We must be able to provide access to our systems and information but in a secure manner. It is imperative that these vital TCI resources be protected to the maximum extent possible but consistent with cost-effective operation.

The protection of our systems and information can be accomplished only through an effective and efficient information systems security (InfoSec) program. We have begun an aggressive effort to build such a program.

This directive is the roadmap to our InfoSec program and the continued success of TCI. For the InfoSec program to be successful, you must give it your full support. Your support is vital to ensure that TCI continues to grow and maintain its leadership role in the widget industry.

(signed by the TCI president and CEO)

TCI InfoSec Requirements and Policy Directive (IRPD)

The TCI InfoSec policy is set forth in the TCI InfoSec requirements and policy directive (TCI InfoSec-P-001). This directive follows the standard format for TCI policies and includes the following:

1. Introduction section, which includes some history as to the need for InfoSec at TCI;
2. Purpose section, which describes why the document exists;
3. Scope section, which defines the breadth of the directive;
4. Responsibilities, which defines and identifies the responsibilities at all levels, including executive management, organizational managers, systems custodians, IT personnel, and users. The directive also will include the requirements for customers', subcontractors', and vendors' access to TCI systems and information;
5. Requirements section, which includes the requirements for

    Identifying the value of the information,

    Access to the TCI systems,

    Access to specific applications and files,

    Audit trails and their review,

    Reporting responsibilities and action to be taken in the event of an indication of a possible violation,

Minimum protection requirements for the hardware, firmware, and software,[3]

Requirements for InfoSec procedures at a TCI department and lower level.

InfoSec Procedures

Based on the TCI InfoSec policy and as stated in the IRPD, each department must establish procedures, based on its unique environment, number of systems, types of configurations, hardware, software, types of information, and the value of the information under its responsibility.

The TCI culture is such that the protection of the information systems and the information they store, process, and transmit is the obligation of every TCI employee. The managers of TCI are required, based on their management positions, to protect the assets of TCI. Therefore, the ISSO reasoned and executive management agreed, each department should comply with the IRPD based on that department's unique position with TCI. Thus, they were to document the methods used to comply with the IRPD through their internal department InfoSec procedural directive. This had several advantages:

1. TCI managers were in a better position to write the document and develop cost-effective procedures that worked for them;
2. It made the department, especially the managers, responsible for compliance with the IRPD;
3. It negated the managers' complaints that their situation was unique and therefore they could not comply with all aspects of an InfoSec procedure (one written by the ISSO), as written;
4. It took this level of detailed InfoSec responsibility off the shoulders of the ISSO and placed it squarely where it belonged, on the managers.

Physical Security

The physical security functions, for the most part, fall under the security department. The Director of Security and the ISSO agreed that the physical security program, as it related to InfoSec, was to remain under the purview of the security department; however, those aspects related to InfoSec would be coordinated with the ISSO or the ISSO's designated representative.

---

[3]The physical security aspects of the requirements would have been coordinated with the applicable security department managers, because they have the responsibility for the physical security of TCI assets. The ISSO's rationale was that physical security should be addressed in this document because it a basic protection process. The Director of Security agreed and approved that process.

The technical countermeasures program relating to emanations of systems' signals or covert signals that may be placed in TCI's sensitive processing areas initially had been placed under the purview of the ISSO; however, the Director of Security became concerned because the systems permeate TCI, which appeared to give the ISSO a great deal of authority. The ISSO's authority for physical security related to systems' facilities, which the Director equated with *power*, was relinquished by the ISSO. The ISSO's rationale was this:

1. It showed the executive management and the Director of Security that the ISSO was interested in getting the job done right and not who had the authority to do it;
2. This move, coupled with the InfoSec procedures responsibility placed on TCI managers, gave clear indication to everyone that the ISSO was interested in getting the job done in a cooperative effort, where InfoSec responsibilities belonged to everyone in a true teamwork effort;
3. It took a heavy responsibility off the shoulders of the ISSO, who no longer was responsible for the physical security aspects and could direct attention to more technical aspects of the InfoSec program, those more enjoyable to the ISSO.

The agreement reached by the ISSO and Director of Security was for the security department to be responsible for

1. Physical access controls to information systems throughout TCI;
2. Physical access control badge readers to areas containing sensitive information processing activities;
3. Physical disconnection of all systems processing information so sensitive that the information could not be processed outside specified areas;
4. Review, analysis, and action related to physical access controls' audit trails;
5. Physical access control of all visitors, vendors, subcontractors, customers, maintenance personnel, and escorting of such personnel into sensitive information processing areas.

Awareness Program

The TCI ISSO decided to concentrate, as a high priority, on the TCI awareness program (a major function under the TCI InfoSec program) because of the need to gain the user support in the protection of TCI information and systems.

The ISSO reasoned that, once the TCI InfoSec policies and baseline procedures were developed and published, the employees must be made aware of them and why they were necessary. Only with the full support and cooperation of the TCI employees could a successful InfoSec Program be established and maintained.

The awareness program process was broken into two major parts: awareness briefings and continuous awareness material.

Awareness Briefings

The awareness briefings included information relative to the need for information and systems protection, the impact of protecting and not protecting the systems and information, and an explanation of the TCI InfoSec program.

The ISSO reasoned that the awareness material and briefings, when given as a general briefing, could be used only for new employees. The general briefings failed to provide the specific information required by various groups of systems users. Therefore, the awareness briefings were tailored to specific audiences as follows:

1. All newly hired employees, whether or not they used a system; the rationale was that all employees handle information and come in contact with computer and telecommunication systems in one form or another;
2. Managers;
3. System users;
4. Information technology department personnel;
5. Engineers;
6. TCI manufacturing personnel;
7. Accounting and Finance personnel;
8. Procurement personnel;
9. Human Resources personnel;
10. Security and Audit personnel;
11. The system security custodians (those with the day-to-day responsibility to ensure that the systems and information were protected in accordance with the InfoSec policy and procedures).

A process was established to identify these personnel, enter their profile information into a database, and using a standard format, track their awareness briefing attendance, both their initial briefings and annual rebriefings. This information also would be used to provide them, through the TCI mail system, awareness material.

Awareness Material

The ISSO, in concert with the Human Resources and Training personnel, decided that ensuring that employees were aware of their InfoSec responsibilities would require constant reminder. After all, InfoSec is not the major function of most of the TCI employees; however, a way must be found to remind the employees that it is a *part* of their major function.

It was decided that awareness material could be provided the employees cost-effectively through

1.   Annual calendars,
2.   Posters,
3.   Labels for systems and diskettes,
4.   Articles published in the TCI publications such as the weekly newsletter,
5.   Log-on notices and system broadcast messages, especially of InfoSec changes.

Although not all-inclusive, the ISSO believed that this TCI InfoSec Awareness program baseline was a good start that could be analyzed for cost-effective improvements at the end of the calendar year.

Access Control and Access Control Systems

Access Control

The ISSO determined that the access control and access control systems ranked as high priorities in establishing processes for the control of access to systems as well as to the information stored, processed, and transmitted by those systems. Therefore, access controls were divided into two sections: access to systems and access to the information on the systems.

The ISSO reasoned that each department created and used the TCI systems and its information. Therefore, the departments should be responsible for controlling access to those systems and information.

The major systems, such as TCI's wide area network, was owned and operated by the IT department whereas individual systems and LANs were owned and operated by the individual departments.

As part of the InfoSec program, the TCI, in coordination with other departments' managers, established a process for all TCI employees who required access to the systems to perform their jobs and would have to obtain system access approval from the manager or a designated representative of that system. The owners' approval was based on a justified need for access as stated by the employee's manager. If the system owner agreed, access was granted.

The ISSO had found, during the initial evaluation of the InfoSec of TCI, that departments had logically grouped their information into categories. They had done so to control access to their own files. This made it easy for the ISSO, because the managers of the departments agreed that, once access to systems was granted by the systems' owners, access to the information on those systems should be approved by the owners of those groups of files, databases, and the like. Therefore, the access control process included a justification by an employee's manager stating not only what systems access were needed and why, but also what information was required for employees to perform their jobs.

For the most part, this was an easy and logical process. For example, in the Accounting Department, personnel generally had access to groups of files and databases based on their job functions, such as accounts payable or accounts receivable.

This access control process helped maintain an audit trail of who approved access to whom and for what purposes. It also helped provide a separation of functions, which is a vital component of any InfoSec program; for example, Accounts Payable personnel should not also handle Accounts Receivable and the invoice processing. Such a system would allow one person too much control over a process, which could be—and has been—used for committing fraud.

The benefit of this process to the ISSO was that it documented an informal process that, for the most part, had been in place. It also placed responsibility for InfoSec of systems and information access exactly where it belonged, with the identified owners of the systems and information.

Once, an ISSO found that one manager did not want to take responsibility for a LAN in the department, and because the information was used by others outside the department, the manager did not want to take ownership of the information. The manager thought the IT department should be the owner; after all, it was responsible for the maintenance of the system.

The ISSO, in this case, asked the manager if the ISSO could be responsible as the owner of the systems and the information. The manager quickly agreed. The ISSO then told the manager that, because it was now owned by the InfoSec organization, access would be denied to the systems and information to all those not in the InfoSec organization.

The manager objected stating that the personnel in his organization needed access to those systems and its information to perform their jobs. After further discussion, the organizational manager agreed that his organization would appear to be the logical owners and subsequently accepted that responsibility.

Access Control Systems

The ISSO, in coordination with the IT, security, and audit departments, determined that the access control systems (hardware and software) belonged to the departments and organizations identified as system owners. However, InfoSec personnel would establish the detailed procedures for the access control systems and compliance with those procedures would be evaluated by the auditors.

The system owners agreed to this process and also to appointing primary and alternate system custodians, who would be responsible for ensuring the TCI InfoSec policies and procedures were followed by all those who used the systems. In addition, the custodian would review the system audit trails, which were mandatory on all TCI systems.[4]

Evaluation of All Hardware, Firmware, and Software

All new hardware, firmware, and software had to be evaluated for any possible impact on the security of the information and systems. This was determined in joint agreement between the ISSO and the IT department personnel, auditors, and security personnel.

To effectively perform this function with a minimal impact on costs and installation schedules, it was determined that a baseline checklist would be developed and that checklist completed by the suppliers of the product, in concert with the InfoSec staff. Any items having an adverse impact on InfoSec would be evaluated based on a risk assessment, using the approved risk management and reporting process.

The process included completion of the baseline InfoSec checklist document and a technical evaluation by InfoSec personnel in concert with IT personnel. If the item (hardware, software, etc.) was considered *risk acceptable*, it was approved for purchase.

If not risk acceptable, the risk management process identified countermeasures. Although this process generally approved the purchase of items, some items could have an unacceptable level of risk but still would be accepted due to their value to TCI. In those instances, special audit trails could be created to monitor the use of the item. In any case, the ISSO understood that it always is better to at least know that a system is vulnerable than to not know of the vulnerability until it is too late.

Risk Management Program

The objective of TCI's risk management program is to *maximize security and minimize cost through risk management.*

To understand the risk management methodology, one must first understand what the term means. *Risk management* is defined as the total process of identifying, controlling, and eliminating or minimizing uncertain events that may affect system resources. This includes risk assessments; risk analyses, including cost-benefit analyses; target selection;

---

[4] At first, the audit trails requirement was to be applied only to those TCI systems processing sensitive TCI information; however, it was quickly discovered that all systems, due to their networking, fell under that category. TCI management agreed that the additional cost of such a requirement was beneficial to TCI, based on the risks of loss of such information by internal or external threats.

implementation and testing; security evaluation of safeguards; and overall InfoSec review.

Risk Assessments

The process of identifying InfoSec risks, determining their magnitude, and identifying areas needing safeguards is called *risk assessment.* In other words, you assess the risk of a particular target, such as a new software application's impact on the system's security processes, architecture, and the like.

The risk assessment process is subdivided into threats, vulnerability, and risks.

Threats are human-made or natural occurrences that could cause adverse affects to systems and information when combined with specific vulnerabilities. For example,

1. Natural threats include such things as fire, floods, hurricanes, and earthquakes;
2. Human-made threats or threat-related matters include such things as unauthorized system access, hacker or cracker or phreaker programs, the perpetrators themselves, theft of systems or services, denial of services, and destruction of systems or information.

Vulnerabilities refer to weaknesses that allow specific threats to cause adverse affects to systems and information. For example,

1. Lack of audit trails;
2. Lack of information backups;
3. Lack of access controls;
4. Anything that weakens the security of the systems and the information they process, store, or transmit.

Risks are the chances that a specific threat can take advantage of a specific vulnerability to cause adverse affects to systems and information. For example,

1. In a strong earthquake area, chances are that systems will be damaged by a strong earthquake;
2. If you do not have audit trails on your system and the system contains company information that would be of value to others, the chances are someone would try to steal that information, and without the audit trail logs, you would not know if someone had tried to penetrate your system, or worse yet, whether he or she succeeded.

Assessments are an evaluation of the threats and vulnerabilities to determine the level of risk to your systems or information that the systems store, process, or transmit. Assessments usually are done through qualitative or quantitative analyses, or a combination of the two. It is the measurement of risks.

Qualitative analyses usually categorize risk as high, medium, or low. It is an "educated best guess," based primarily on opinions of knowledgeable others gathered through interviews, history, tests, and the experience of the person doing the assessment.

Quantitative analyses usually use statistical sampling based on mathematical computations determining the probability of an adverse occurrence based on historical data. It still is an "educated best guess," but based primarily on statistical results.

Risk Analyses

Analyses of the risks, the countermeasures to mitigate those risks, and the cost-benefit ratios associated with those risks and countermeasures make up the risk analyses process, which basically is risk assessment with the cost and benefit factors added.

The Risk Management Process

The goal of the risk management process, of course, is to provide the best protection of systems and the information they store, process, or transmit at the lowest cost consistent with the value of the systems and the information.

Remember that the InfoSec program is a company program made up of professionals who provide service and support to the company. Therefore, the risk management process must be based on the needs of TCI customers. Also, be sure that the risk management concepts, program, and processes are used informally and formally in all aspects of the InfoSec program, including when and how to do awareness briefings, the impact of information systems security policies and procedures on the employees, and so forth.

The following steps should be considered in the ISSO's process:

1. *Management Interest.* Identify areas of major interest to executive management and customers and approach them from a business point of view. So, the process should begin with interviews of internal customers to determine what areas of InfoSec are adversely affecting their operations the most. Target those areas first, as the starting point for the risk management program.
2. *Identify Specific Targets.* These targets would include software applications, hardware, telecommunications, electronic media storage, and so forth.
3. *Input Sources.* These include users, system administrators, auditors, security officers, technical journals, technical bulletins, CERT alerts (Internet), risk assessment application programs, and so on.

4.   *Identify Potential Threats.* These may be internal or external, natural or human-made.
5.   *Identify Vulnerabilities.* Do this through interviews, experience, history, testing.
6.   *Risk Identification.* Match threats to vulnerabilities with existing countermeasures, verify, and validate.
7.   *Assess Risks.* Are they acceptable or not acceptable? Identify residual risk, then certify the process and gain approval. If the risks are not acceptable, identify countermeasures; identify each countermeasure's cost; and compare countermeasures, risks, and costs to mitigated risks.

Recommendations to Management

When the risk assessment or risk analysis is completed, the ISSO must make recommendations to management. Remember, in making recommendations, to think from a business point of view: cost, benefits, profits, public relations, and so forth.

Risk Management Reports

A briefing that includes a formal written report is the vehicle to bring the risks to management's attention. The report should identify areas that need improvement, those performing well, and recommended actions for improvement, including costs and benefits.

Remember that it is management's decision to accept or mitigate the risks and how much to spend to do so. The ISSO is the specialist, the in-house consultant. Management has responsibility to decide what to do. It may follow your recommendations, ignore them, or take some other action. In any case, the ISSO has provided the service and support required.

If the decision is made that no action will be taken, conducting the analyses still provides a benefit. The ISSO now has a better understanding of the environment, as well as some areas of vulnerability. This information will still help in managing an InfoSec program.

Security Tests and Evaluations Program

The security tests and evaluations (ST&E) program was looked at by the ISSO as a needed process once the TCI InfoSec program processes of awareness, access control, and risk management were implemented.

The ST&E function's process was developed to incorporate testing and evaluating of total InfoSec processes, environments, hardware, software, and firmware, as a proactive method to support risk assessment and the evaluations of the systems' components.

The ISSO believed that the auditors' compliance audits were more of a checklist process of ensuring compliance with TCI InfoSec policies and procedures. What was needed, the ISSO reasoned, was a process to actually test InfoSec processes, systems, and the like, to determine if they were meeting the InfoSec needs of TCI—regardless of whether they complied with the InfoSec policies and procedures.

For example, the ST&E program would include periodically obtaining a user ID on a system with various access privileges. The InfoSec staff member, using that identification, would violate that system and attempt to gain unauthorized access to various files, databases, and systems. That information was analyzed in concert with a comparison of the systems' audit trails, thus profiling the InfoSec of a system or network. Also, the ST&E program would include a review of records and prior audit trail documents to help establish the "InfoSec environment" being tested and evaluated.

Noncompliance Inquiries

Noncompliance inquiries (NCI) were identified as an InfoSec responsibility and the process was developed by the InfoSec staff and coordinated with the audit and security management. The NCI process is as follows:

1. Receive allegations of noncompliance by auditors, security personnel, managers, users, and generally anyone else;
2. Evaluate the allegation and, if not considered acceptable, file it;[5]
3. Conduct an inquiry if the allegation is substantiated, including interviews, technical reviews, document reviews, and so on;
4. Analyze the information gathered, collate it, and provide a formal report to management with copies to the appropriate departments, such as security and human resources;
5. Protect the report for reasons of privacy and include recommendations and trend analyses to mitigate future occurrences.

Contingency Planning and Disaster Recovery Program

A contingency planning and disaster recovery (CP-DR) system is one of the least difficult programs to establish and, yet, always seems to be a difficult task to accomplish. With the change in information systems' environments and configurations (e.g., client servers, LANs, distributed processing), this problem may be getting worse.

Prior to discussing CP-DR, it is important to understand why it is needed. It really is a very important aspect of an InfoSec program and may

---

[5] The ISSO is sensitive to privacy issues and does not want to initiate an inquiry without substantiated information, because someone may have a grudge against another and use the process to harass that person.

even be its most vital part. The ISSO must remember that the purpose of InfoSec is to

1.   Minimize the probability of security vulnerabilities,
2.   Minimize the damage if such vulnerability is exploited,
3.   *Provide a method to recover from the damage efficiently and effectively.*

What Is It?

A *contingency plan* is a strategy for responding to emergencies, backup operations, and recovering after a disaster; it addresses what action will be taken to return to normal operations. Emergencies requiring action would include such natural acts as floods or earthquakes and human-caused acts such as fires or hacker attacks causing denial of services. *Disaster recovery* is the restoration of the information systems, facility, or other related assets following a significant disruption of services.

Why Do It?

The question is often asked, primarily by users, why a CP-DR program is necessary. Everyone associated with using, protecting, and maintaining information systems and the information they store, process, or transmit must understand the need for such a program. It is to

1.   Assist in protecting vital information,
2.   Minimize the adverse impact on productivity,
3.   Stay in business.

How Do You Do It?

Each CP-DR program is unique to the environment, culture, and philosophy of each business or government agency. However, the basic program, regardless of business or agency, requires the development and maintenance of a CP-DR plan. It must be periodically tested, problems identified and corrected, and processes changed to support minimizing the chances of adverse events happening again.

The CP-DR Planning System

The CP-DR plan must be written, based on the standard format used by TCI. The following generic format is offered for consideration:

1.   *Purpose.* State the reason for the plan and its objective. This should be specific enough so that it is clear to all who read it why it has been written.
2.   *Scope.* State the scope and applicability of the plan. Does it include all systems, all locations, subcontractors?

3. *Assumptions.* State the top priorities, the support promised, and the incidents to be included and excluded. For example, if your area has no typhoons, will you assume that typhoons, as a potential disaster threat, will not be considered?

4. *Responsibilities.* State who is to be responsible for taking what action. This should be stated clearly, so everyone knows who is responsible for what. Consider a generic breakdown, such as managers, systems administrators, users, and so on. Also, specific authority and responsibility should be listed by a person's title and not necessarily his or her name. This approach will save time in updating the plan due to people changing jobs.

5. *Strategy.* Discuss backup requirements and how often they should be accomplished based on classification of information; state how you will recover and so on.

6. *Personnel.* Maintain an accurate, complete, and current list of key CP-DR personnel, including addresses, phone numbers, pager numbers, cellular phone numbers, and the like. Be sure to establish an emergency priority notification list and a list of response teams' members and how to contact them in an emergency.

7. *Information.* Maintain an on-site inventory list and an off-site inventory list and identify the rotation process to ensure a history and current inventory of files. Identify vital information. This information must come from the owner of that information and be classified according to its importance, based on approved guidelines.

8. *Hardware.* Maintain an inventory list, including suppliers' names, serial numbers, property identification numbers, and so on; ensure emergency replacement contracts are in place; and maintain hardcopies of applicable documents on and off site.

9. *Software.* Identify and maintain backup operating systems and application systems software. This should include original software and at least one backup copy of each. Be sure to identify the version numbers and so forth. In this way, you can compare what is listed in the plan with what actually is installed. It would not be the first time that software backups were not kept current and compatible with the hardware; thus systems were not able to process, store, and transmit much-needed information.

10. *Documentation.* All important documentation should be identified, listed, inventoried, and maintained current in both on- and off-site locations.

11. *Telecommunications.* The identification and maintenance of telecommunications hardware and software listings are vital if you are operating in any type of network environment. Many systems today cannot operate in a stand-alone configuration; therefore, the telecommunications lines, backups, schematics, and the like are of vital importance to getting back in operation within the time period

required. As with other documentation, the identification, listing, and so forth should be maintained at multiple on- and off-site locations. Be sure to identify all emergency requirements and all alternate communication methods.

12. *Supplies.* Supplies often are forgotten when establishing a CP-DR plan, as they take a "backseat" to hardware and software. However, listing and maintenance of vital supplies are required, including the names, addresses, telephone numbers, and contracts information concerning the providers of those supplies. Be sure to store sufficient quantities at appropriate locations on- and off-site. If you think this is an unimportant matter, try using a printer when its toner cartridge has dried out or is empty. Physical supplies for consideration should include plastic tarps to cover systems from water damage in the event of a fire when sprinkler systems are activated.

13. *Transportation and Equipment.* If you have a disaster or emergency requiring the use of a backup facility or need backup copies of software and the like, you obviously must have transportation and the applicable equipment (e.g., a dolly for hauling heavy items) to do the job. Therefore, you must plan for such things. List emergency transportation needs and sources. State how you will obtain emergency transportation and equipment and which routes and alternate routes to take to the off-site location. Be sure to include maps in the vehicles and also in the plan. Be sure fully-charged, handheld fire extinguishers are available that will work on various types of fires, such as electrical, paper, and chemical.

14. *Processing Locations.* Many businesses and agencies sign contractual agreements to ensure that they have an appropriate off-site location to be used in the event their facility cannot support their activities. Ensure that emergency processing agreements are in place that will provide you with top-priority service and support in the event of an emergency or disaster. Even then, you may have a difficult time using the facility if the disaster is a large-scale disaster and others also have contracted for the facility. Be sure periodically to use the facility to ensure that you can process, store, or transmit information at that location. Do not forget to identify on-site locations that can be used or converted for use in the event of other than a total disaster.

15. *Utilities.* Identify on-site and off-site emergency power needs and locations. Do not forget that these requirements change as facilities, equipment, and hardware changes. Battery power and uninterruptable power might not be able to carry the load or be too old to even work. These must be tested periodically. As with the printer cartridge supplies, systems without power are useless. In addition to power, do not forget the air conditioning requirements. It would be important to know how long a system can process without air conditioning based on certain temperature and humidity readings.

16.   *Documentation.* Identify all related documentation, store it in multiple on- and off-site locations, and be sure to include the CP-DR plan.
17.   *Other.* Miscellaneous items not already covered.

Test the Plan

There is no use in having a plan that has not been tested, for only through testing can the ISSO determine that the plan will work when required. Therefore, it must be tested periodically. The plan need not be tested all at once, because that would probably cause a loss of productivity by the employees, which would not be cost-effective.

It is best to test the plan in increments, relying on all the pieces to fit together when all the parts have been tested. Regardless of when and how you test the plan, which is a management decision, it must be tested. Probably the best way to determine how and what to test and in what order is to set priorities for testing based on the priorities of assets.

When testing, the scenarios used should be as realistic as possible. This should include emergency response, testing backup applications and systems, and recovery operations.

Through testing, document the problems and areas of vulnerability identified. Determine why they occurred and establish formal projects to fix each problem. Additionally, make whatever cost-effective process changes are necessary to ensure that the same problem would not happen again or the chance of it happening is minimized.

SUMMARY

1.   Establishing the proper InfoSec functions in the right priority order is vital to establishing the InfoSec program baseline.
2.   The InfoSec functional processes generally should follow the function descriptions noted in the ISSO's charter of responsibilities.
3.   Establishing a process to determine the categories of information identified by the general value of that information will assist in the development of a cost-effective InfoSec program.
4.   The functions and processes that should be developed first are the InfoSec policies and procedures documentation, an InfoSec awareness program, and an access control program.
5.   The functions to closely follow (assuming limited resources for parallel work) are those related to system evaluations, noncompliance inquiries, and contingency planning and disaster recovery.

10

Metrics Management

CHAPTER OBJECTIVE

The objective of this chapter is to describe and discuss the identification, development, and use of metrics charts to assist in managing an InfoSec program. This chapter is designed to provide the basic guidance necessary for the development of a metrics methodology to understand what, why, when, and how InfoSec can be measured. Using the fictitious company (TCI) and functions described previously, a metrics system will be developed. The chapter includes a discussion of how to use metrics to brief management, justify budget expenses, and use trend analyses to develop a more efficient and effective InfoSec program.

WHAT IS A METRIC?

To begin to understand how to use metrics to support the management of an InfoSec program, it is important to understand what we mean by *metrics*. For our purposes, a *metric* is defined as a standard of measurement using quantitative, statistical, or mathematical analyses. In an InfoSec program, metric refers to the application of quantitative, statistical, or mathematical analyses to measuring InfoSec functional trends and workload.

WHAT IS INFOSEC METRICS MANAGEMENT?

InfoSec metrics management is the managing of an InfoSec program through the use of metrics. Metrics can be used where managerial tasks must be demonstrated for such purposes as supporting the ISSO's position on budget matters, justifying the cost-effectiveness of decisions, or determining the impact of downsizing on providing service and support to customers.

The primary process to collect metrics is as follows:

1.   Identify each InfoSec function;[1]
2.   Determine what drives that function, such as labor (number of people or workhours used), policies, procedures, and systems;
3.   Establish a metrics collection process, which could be as simple as filling out a log for later summarization and analyses or a spreadsheet that can automatically incorporate InfoSec statistics into graphs (the preferred method), which will make it easier for the ISSO to use the metrics for supporting management decisions or during briefings.

The decision to establish a process to collect statistics relative to a particular InfoSec function should be decided by answering the following questions:

1.   Why should these statistics be collected?
2.   What specific statistics will be collected?
3.   How will these statistics be collected?
4.   When will these statistics be collected?
5.   Who will collect these statistics?
6.   Where (at what point in the function's process) will these statistics be collected?

By answering these questions, the ISSO can better *think out* the process of whether or not a metrics collection process should be established for a particular function. This thought-out process will be useful in helping explain its use to the InfoSec staff or management, if necessary. Such reasoning also will help the ISSO decide whether or not to continue maintaining a particular metric after a specific period of time.

All metrics should be reviewed, evaluated, and reconsidered for continuation at the end of each year. Remember, although the collection of the metrics information will help the ISSO better manage the InfoSec responsibilities, a cost is incurred in the collection and maintenance of these metrics in terms of resources (people who collect, enter, process, print, and maintain the metrics for you, as well as the hardware and software used to support that effort).

The chart format and colors sometimes are dictated by management; however, the options of what type of charts to use to depict what is best for analyses or presentation to management is probably up to the ISSO.

---

[1] Performance of each function is assumed to cost time, money, and equipment.

The ISSO should experiment with various types of line, bar, and pie charts. It is recommended that the charts be kept simple and easy to understand. Remember the old saying, *"A picture is worth a thousand words."* The charts should need very little explanation.

If the ISSO will use the charts for briefings, the briefing should only comment on the different trends. The reason for this is to clearly and concisely present the material and not get bogged down in details that distract from the objective of the charts.

One way to determine if the message the charts are trying to portray is clear is to have someone look at the charts and describe what it tells. If it tells what the chart is supposed to portray, then no changes are needed. If not, the ISSO should then ask what the chart does seem to represent and what leads the person to that conclusion. The ISSO must then rework the chart until the message is clear and it shows exactly what the ISSO wants the chart to show.

The following are some basic examples of InfoSec metrics that can be collected to assist an ISSO in managing an InfoSec program.

METRICS SHOWING THE INFOSEC DRIVERS

There are two basic InfoSec drivers within an organization; that is, those things that cause the InfoSec workload to be what it is, to increase or decrease:

1. The number of systems that fall under the purview of the InfoSec Program,
2. The number of users of those systems.

A question must be asked: Why are these metrics worth tracking? Are they worth tracking because they drive the InfoSec workload, which means they drive the number of hours that the InfoSec staff must expend in meeting the InfoSec responsibilities relative to those systems and users?

As the number of users on TCI networks change or the number of systems change, so does the workload; therefore, so does the number of staff members required and the amount of budget required. For example, assume that TCI is downsizing— not an unusual occurrence, which ISSOs eventually will face in their InfoSec careers. If the ISSO knows that TCI will downsize its workforce by 10% and assuming that all in the workforce use computers, (not an unusual occurrence in today's workforce), the workload also should decrease about 10%. This may cause the ISSO to also downsize (lay off staff) by approximately 10%.

However, the downsizing, whether it be more or less than the TCI average, should be based on the related InfoSec workload. The InfoSec drivers are metrics that can help the ISSO determine the probable impact of the TCI downsizing on the InfoSec program and organization. The metrics associated with that effort also can justify downsizing decisions to TCI management, including possibly downsizing by 5% instead of 10%.

One thing the ISSO must remember is that the use of metrics is a tool to support many of the ISSO decisions and actions; however, it is not perfect. Therefore, the ISSO must make some assumptions that may relate to the statistical data to be collected. That is fine. The ISSO must remember that metrics is not rocket science, only a tool to help the ISSO take better informed actions and make better informed decisions. So, the ISSO should never get carried away with the hunt for "perfect statistics."

The spreadsheets and graphs used for metrics management can become very complicated, with links to other spreadsheets, elaborate three-D graphics, and the like. This may work for some, but the ISSO should consider the KISS (keep it simple, stupid) principle when collecting and maintaining metrics. This is true especially if the ISSO is just getting started and has no or very little experience with metrics. One may find that the project leaders who are developing the "automated statistical collection" application are expending more hours developing an application that never seems to work just quite right than it takes to calculate the statistics by hand.

It also is important, from a managerial viewpoint, that all charts, statistics, and spreadsheets be done in a standard format. This is necessary so that they can be ready at all times for reviews and briefings to upper management. This standard is indicative of a professional organization and one that is operating as a focused team.

Those ISSOs who are new to the position or management in general may think that this is somewhat ridiculous. After all, what difference does it make as long as the information is as accurate as possible and provides the necessary information? One may be correct, but in the business environment, standards, consistency, and indications of teamwork always are a concern of management.

The ISSO job and management support are hard enough to get and maintain; do not make it more difficult than it has to be. Another negative impact concerning nonconformance of format will be that the charts will be the topic of discussions and not the information on them. Once the nonconformance to briefing charts' standards is discussed, management already has formed a negative bias. Therefore, anything presented will make it more difficult to get the point across, gain the decision desired, and meet the established objective of the briefing.

It is better to just follow the standards that are set than to argue their validity. It is better to save the energy for arguing for those things that are more important. After all, one cannot win and the ISSO does not want to be looked at as "a non-team player."

Of course, the number, type, collection methods, and so on that the ISSO will use will depend on the environment and the ISSO's ability to cost-effectively collect and maintain the metrics. Next is an example of general metrics that may be used based on the duties, responsibilities, and functions of the TCI ISSO.

EXAMPLE

As an ISSO, you decided that it would be a good idea to use the drivers metric, which is used to track the number of systems and users of the systems. You made that decision based on answering the how, what, why, when, who, and where questions noted previously.

1. Why Should These Statistics Be Collected?

The drivers metrics, which tracks the number of users and systems for which the ISSO has InfoSec responsibility, is required to assist in supporting the head count budget for those users and systems performing the following functions:

Access control,

Audit trail analyses,

Compliance inspections,

Systems' approvals,

Awareness briefings,

Contingency planning and disaster recovery.

2. What Specific Statistics Will Be Collected?

Statistics will be collected on total users and total systems.

3. How Will These Statistics Be Collected?

The statistics on total users will be collected by totaling the number of user IDs on each network system and adding to it the number of stand-alone systems. Each stand-alone system is assumed to have only one user.

Each stand-alone microcomputer and each networked system (each will count as one system) will be identified and totaled using the approved system documentation on file within the InfoSec organization on the approved systems database. At TCI, all systems processing sensitive TCI information, falling within the categories previously recognized at TCI for identifying information by its value, must be approved by the ISSO (or designated InfoSec staff members). Therefore, data collection is available through InfoSec organization's records.

4. When Will These Statistics Be Collected?

The statistics will be compiled on the first business day of each month and incorporated into the InfoSec drivers graph maintained on the InfoSec department's administrative microcomputer.

5. Who Will Collect These Statistics?

The statistics will be collected, entered, and maintained by the project leaders responsible for system accesses and system approvals.

6. Where (at What Point in the Function's Process) Will These Statistics Be Collected?

The collection of statistics will be based on the information available and on file in the InfoSec organization through close of business on the last business day of the month.

SIGNIFICANCE OF THE TOTAL SYSTEMS CHART

The number of systems is a driver of InfoSec workload because the InfoSec functions' level of effort (LOE) and some projects are based on the number of systems. These include the following:

1. The InfoSec staff must support the IT department's installation and maintenance of the systems;
2. The systems must be approved to process, store, and transmit sensitive TCI information;
3. The access control systems must be installed and maintained on each system;
4. Contingency planning and disaster recovery processes must be modified to integrate each system into the plans.

The chart in Figures 10.1 and 10.2 can be used by the ISSO for the following:

1. To justify the need for more budget and other resources,
2. To indicate that the InfoSec program is operating more efficiently because the budget and other resources have not increased although the number of systems has increased,
3. To help justify why budget and other resources cannot be decreased.

SIGNIFICANCE OF THE NEW SYSTEMS AND USERS CHARTS

The number of systems' users is another driver of InfoSec workload, because the InfoSec functions' LOE and some projects are based on the number of users. These include the following:

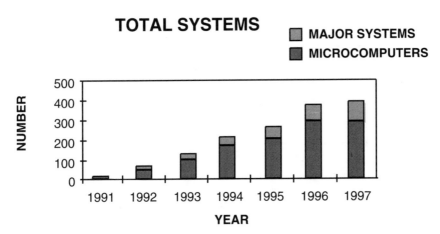

Figure 10.1   What a total systems tracking chart may look like when the tracking occurs over several years.

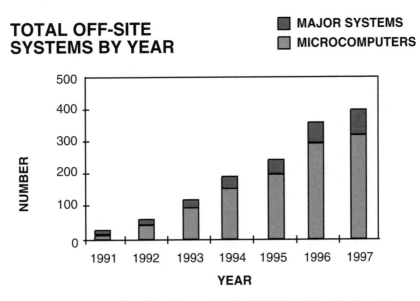

Figure 10.2   A similar chart, but this tracks the TCI off-site location's systems.

1. The InfoSec staff provide access controls for users,
2. The number of non-compliance inquiries probably will increase based on the increased number of users,
3. The time to review audit trail records will increase due to more activity because of more users,
4. The number of awareness briefings and processing of additional awareness material will increase due to an increase in users.

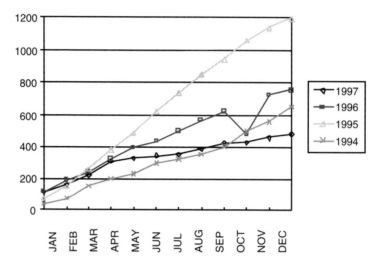

Figure 10.3   A monthly tracking of the number of new systems users added to TCI systems over a four-year period.

The chart in Figure 10.3 can be used by the ISSO for the following:

1.   To justify the need for more budget and other resources,
2.   To indicate that the InfoSec program is operating more efficiently because the budget and other resources have not increased although the number of systems have increased,
3.   To help justify why budget and other resources cannot be decreased.

NEW USER ACCESS TO SYSTEMS

A major InfoSec service and support function is to add new users to systems and provide them access privileges as directed by their management and information owners. As part of that service and support effort, the ISSO wants to ensure that these users gain access as quickly as possible, because the users cannot perform their jobs without access or new access privileges. If users could not gain expeditious access, then the InfoSec program was costing TCI the lost productivity of these employees or even possibly lost revenue in other forms. The ISSO, in coordination with the InfoSec staff responsible for the access control function, evaluated the access control process and determined that users should gain access within 24 hours of receipt of a request from management.

  The ISSO decided to track this process (Figure 10.4) because of its high visibility. Nothing can damage the InfoSec program faster than a hostile manager whose employees cannot gain systems access to do their work.

ACCOMPLISHED WITHIN 24 HOURS

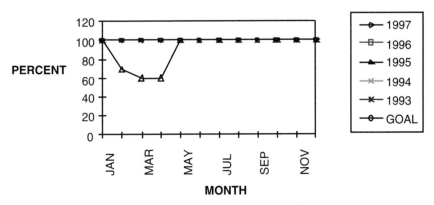

Figure 10.4   The time it takes for a user to gain access following a request by management. In this case, except during the 1995 period (January–May) the goal was met each month of each year. Therefore, the lines are embedded in the 100% goal line and not visible.

EXAMPLES OF OTHER METRICS CHARTS

Numerous metrics charts can be developed to support the various needs of the ISSO. Figures 10.5 through 10.12 show examples of some of those charts.[2] For example, Figure 10.7 shows that the average processing time was well under the goal. The ISSO may consider lowering the goal to offer new challenges to the InfoSec staff.

The ISSO also may use this information when budget cuts are required. Figure 10.7 could be shown to management and modified to show what would happen if the staff were cut by one person, two people, and so on. In other words, the average system approval turnaround time would increase. Management may or may not want to live with those consequences. In most cases, it will say cut anyway.

The chart can show the ISSO where staff cuts can be made and still meet the expected goals. The ISSO also can use this information when deciding to reallocate resources (transfer a person) to a function where the goals are not being met and where the fastest way to meet the goal is to add personnel. A word of caution is needed here: Adding or decreasing personnel usually is considered a fast, simplistic solution; however, it is not always the answer.

---

[2] Try developing other metrics charts and also, using the examples, determine how they could be used to support ISSO requirements, to determine successes and failures of the InfoSec program, and to support briefings.

TOTAL TCI INFOSEC APPROVAL PROCESSING WORKLOAD

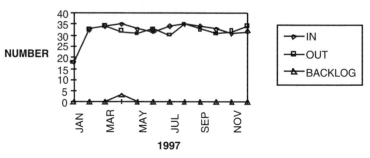

Figure 10.5 Tracking the workload of InfoSec procedure documentation, which is approved by the InfoSec organization prior to processing of TCI sensitive information.

INFOSEC SYSTEM APPROVALS TOTAL AVERAGE PROCESSING TIME

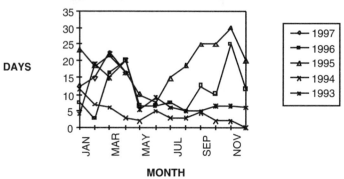

Figure 10.6 A metrics chart showing the average number of days it takes to approve a system for processing sensitive TCI information.

TOTAL AVERAGE PROCESSING TIME

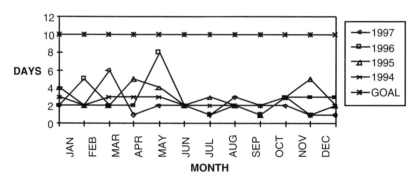

Figure 10.7 Tracking the average system approval processing time against a ten business day goal.

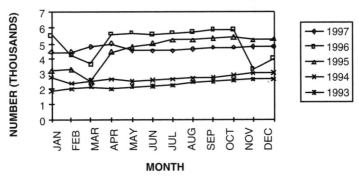

Figure 10.8 Tracking the total number of users given an InfoSec briefing.

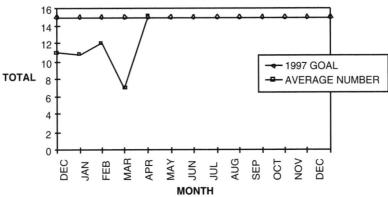

Figure 10.9 Tracking the number of users briefed per briefing. The goal to brief at least 15 persons per briefing as a cost-effective use of the InfoSec staff.

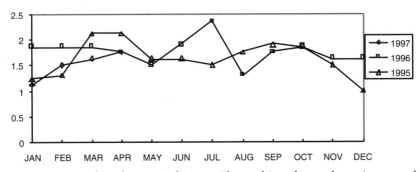

Figure 10.10 Tracking log-on violations. The goal is to lower the ratio as much as possible.

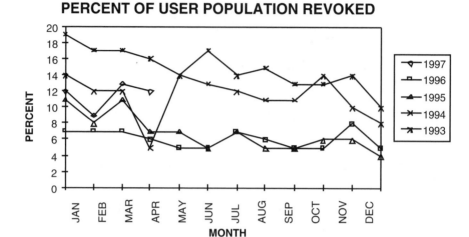

Figure 10.11   Percent of users revoked. The task is to lower the percent as much as possible. Again, this is due to lost time and lost productivity, which translates into costs.

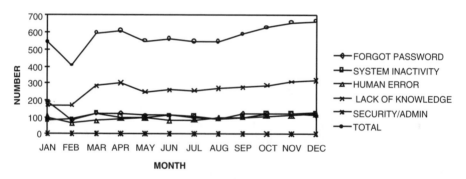

Figure 10.12   Tracking users revoked from the systems. This metric would be analyzed to determine the reason for the revocations with the objective of finding ways to lower that number by looking at the systemic causes.

Many project leaders and ISSOs have found over the years that projects and level of effort problems not always are solved by adding "more bodies" to the problem. First look at the process and systemic problems. This usually is a more cost effective, long-term approach to solving these types of problems.

The log-on violations chart (Figure 10.10) indicates how well users are complying with the InfoSec program requirements. It also indicates some of the costs of that program which can be quantified. The rationale is that violations cause users and the InfoSec staff members time and lost productivity. In addition, failure to follow the requirements may cause increased vulnerabilities; therefore, increased risks to TCI systems and information to denial of service attacks, compromise of sensitive information, and so forth. It also may indicate some level of attacks being made against the system—the most serious problem.

TCI INFOSEC METRIC METHODOLOGY

The ISSO decided to establish a process that would provide guidelines on the need, establishment, and implementation of metrics charts. The ISSO used an InfoSec function to develop the process—the methodology—to achieve the following results (Figure 10.13 shows the results):

1. The TCI InfoSec would conduct security tests and evaluations (ST&E) as prescribed by the TCI InfoSec policies and procedures,
2. Results of the TCI InfoSec ST&E would be charted,
3. Each chart would be evaluated to determine whether a pattern or trend exists,
4. Patterns and trends would be evaluated to determine how effectively a function is being performed,
5. Results and recommendations would be presented, as required by InfoSec policies and procedures, to the applicable managers.

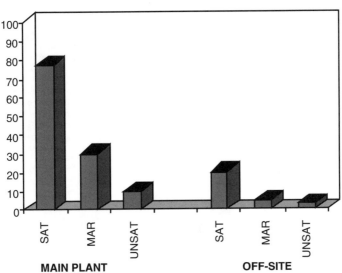

INFOSEC ST&E EVALUATION RATINGS

Figure 10.13   The results of the ST&Es. Additional methods include identifying the results by department, identifying the primary causes of the ratings, and identifying a breakdown of the results by department by deficiencies.

SUMMARY

1. Metrics management is an excellent method to track InfoSec functions related to LOE, costs, use of resources, and the like.
2. The information can be analyzed and the results of the analyses used to identify areas where efficiency improvements are necessary, determine the effectiveness of InfoSec functional goals, be used as input for performance reviews of the InfoSec staff members (a more objective approach than the subjective performance reviews of today's ISSOs), as well as to identify where InfoSec service and support to TCI requires improvement, meets its goals, and so on.

11

Annual Reevaluation and Future Plans

CHAPTER OBJECTIVE

The objective of this chapter is to discuss what to do after the InfoSec program has been implemented; how to determine the InfoSec Program's success and how to plan for the new year.

ONE-YEAR REVIEW

TCI's fiscal year and calendar year both end on December 31. The ISSO decided that the beginning of the fourth quarter (October) is a good time to start planning for the coming year. To plan for the coming year, the ISSO must first determine how successful the InfoSec program has been in the past year. Of interest would be

1. What was accomplished?
2. What was planned but never completed?
3. What was planned but never started?
4. What was successful?
5. What was unsuccessful?
6. Why was it unsuccessful?

LEVEL OF EFFORT ACTIVITIES

Level of effort (LOE) activities are the day-to-day InfoSec activities or functions performed by the InfoSec staff, previously identified as the ISSO responsibilities, such as

1.   Access control;
2.   Awareness program;
3.   Noncompliance inquiries;
4.   Security tests and evaluations program.

The ISSO has asked each LOE leader to evaluate the process used for completing his or her assigned LOE function. This is to be accomplished by each functional team determining what worked, what did not work, how much time was spent on each task or sub-task on average, how could the job be done better, how to change the processes, and what forms used should be modified or eliminated.

The ISSO directed that any recommended changes be quantified in time or cost savings. If the changes could not be so quantified, the staff members would have a difficult time changing the process. The ISSO reasoned that, with few exceptions, changes that did not save time or money probably were not worth making as nonquantified changes cost money with usually no value in return.

The ISSO directed that all members of each function support their functional leader in this endeavor and provide a briefing to be held the first week in November. During that briefing, the functional processes would be discussed and modified where necessary. If the modifications could not be accomplished within 30 days, a formal project plan would have to be developed and briefed at that November meeting.

PROJECTS

During the first week of October, the ISSO began the evaluation of the InfoSec Program for the past year. The ISSO, in concert with the InfoSec staff, reviewed the projects begun that year, as well as those begun the previous year and completed that year.

The ISSO determined the following:

1.   Did each project accomplish its objective?
2.   Was the project completed in accordance with the project plan?
3.   For those projects not completed on time, what caused missing the completion date?
4.   For those projects completed ahead of schedule, what caused the early completion?[1]

---

[1] The ISSO wants this information because it may be due to poor project planning, which must be corrected, or it may be due to a unique approach, which could be used on other programs.

5.   What was the cost of each project?
6.   Were the projected benefits of the projects realized?

The ISSO analyzed all the projects and, based on that evaluation, modified the process used for initiating, determining costs, determining resource allocations, and determining schedules for all new projects.

Once the analysis was complete, the ISSO and staff members determined what new projects would be required for the following year. Those projects, once identified, would be assigned to the applicable member of the staff as the project leader. The staff members then would be given 30 days to complete a draft project plan. The plan is to identify the specific objective to be accomplished, all tasks, milestones, resources required, and the like.

The ISSO scheduled a staff meeting during the first week of November. At that meeting, all the project leaders presented their project plans to the ISSO and the staff for evaluation and discussion. Recommended changes to the project plans were discussed and action taken to change the plans as appropriate.

It is the responsibility of the ISSO to ensure that adequate resources are allocated for the completion of the projects as planned. Where several members of the InfoSec staff are assigned to lead or support projects, the ISSO sets priorities for the projects and allows the project leader and support staff to work out the details. Where conflicts in work arise, the matter is discussed with the ISSO, who makes the final decision based on the input of all concerned.

This approach follows the management philosophy of having decisions made at the lowest possible level where the required information on which to base a decision is known. It also meets the ISSO's philosophy of trusting the professional InfoSec staff.

INFOSEC STRATEGIC, TACTICAL, AND ANNUAL PLANS

Once the ISSO was briefed on the LOE and projects, the results could be mapped against the InfoSec strategic, tactical, and annual plans. If the InfoSec program was successful, the LOE and project results could be identified as some of the specific building blocks of each plan.

The goals of the InfoSec annual plan should have been accomplished. If so, the ISSO would identify the links between the successful accomplishment of those goals with the TCI Annual Business Plan and the TCI and InfoSec strategic and tactical plans as appropriate.

If a direct link between the accomplishments of the InfoSec staff and the goals of the plan cannot be shown, the ISSO must question why the specific projects or LOEs identified were done in the first place. There may be a very valid reason; however, this should always be questioned, as any resource allocations that cannot be directly linked to the accomplishment of stated goals is probably a misallocation of resources. Therefore, it is an added cost burden on the InfoSec budget and additional overhead cost to TCI.

LINKING INFOSEC ACCOMPLISHMENTS TO TCI GOALS

The ISSO believes that the initial reasons for the TCI InfoSec program and TCI's reasons for establishing the ISSO position have not changed, but a reverification and validation probably would be a good idea. To be sure that the InfoSec program and the ISSO's accomplishments are meeting their stated purpose, the ISSO decides on the following course of action:

1. Using a link analysis methodology, the ISSO maps all the LOE and project results to all applicable InfoSec and TCI plans;
2. The ISSO develops a formal presentation to be given to TCI executive management in which the InfoSec program status is briefed (assuming that the ISSO's boss agrees).

The results of the link analysis (Figure 11.1) disclosed that overall the InfoSec program goals, LOE, projects, and objectives, with some minor setbacks and exceptions over the year, were meeting the InfoSec needs of TCI.

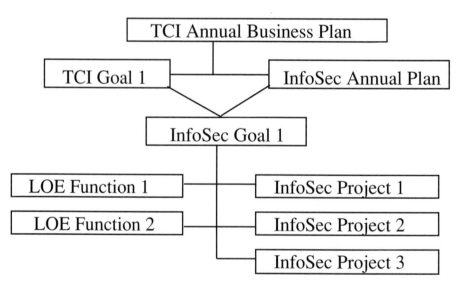

Figure 11.1 How the InfoSec LOE and projects support the InfoSec program and one of TCI's goals.

The ISSO discussed the matter with the Director of IT. The Director agreed that a briefing would be a good idea, especially since this is the end of the first year of the formal InfoSec program. The Director provided several recommendations:

1. The briefing should take no longer than 15 minutes plus 15 minutes for questions;
2. The ISSO should use no technical jargon but speak in business terms of costs, benefits, competitive advantage, and give the TCI management some sense of assurance that the information and systems are being protected as needed;
3. The briefing charts should be clear, concise, and more of a graphical presentation than text;
4. The briefing should be given professionally, objectively, and not be a *soapbox* for requesting additional resources or to show how great a job the ISSO was doing;
5. At least 5 minutes of the 15 minutes should be used to brief on next year's projects, goals, their costs, and how they would benefit TCI.

The ISSO had not been prepared to present the new year's plans and projects as part of the briefing. However, it appeared that the necessary information would be available, based on the previous briefings and discussions with the InfoSec staff.

The ISSO suggested a briefing to be held the first week of December. The Director agreed to set it up. The ISSO's rationale for a meeting in December was that the InfoSec staff's LOE and project input would be available on or about the first week of November and that would provide sufficient time to develop the briefing.

The ISSO wanted to ensure that the briefing accomplished its goals, and that could be jeopardized, not by the material, but by the manner and format used. The ISSO had heard of several briefers having their message ignored because the format, fonts, colors, or whatever used to present the facts was disliked by one or more of the executive managers.

The ISSO knew that such trivia should not be a prime concern to executive management, but the ISSO also knew that such things did occur. To ensure that the InfoSec briefing was successful, the proper format would be the first item of business.

The ISSO stopped by the desks of several of the key executive managers' secretaries who provided insight as to the correct format, font size, and color of slides to use. At the same time, the ISSO was given insight from several of the secretaries as to how to present the material in a manner the executives preferred.

The ISSO long ago learned that the secretaries of executive managers had great insight as to what worked with their bosses and what did not. The ISSO's respect for them and informal assistance over the year had made them "close allies." Now that friendship would help assure a successful briefing.

METRICS ANALYSIS

As part of the year-end review, the ISSO did a complete analysis of the metrics charts developed and used throughout the first year of the InfoSec program. The charts had grown to over 47 separate metrics charts. The ISSO was concerned that some of them had outlived their usefulness, while others continued to be of value.

An analysis of the metrics charts indicated that several were necessary to track particular problem areas. However, the problems appeared to have been resolved and the charts, for the last four months, supported that view.

Some metrics charts were developed and briefed periodically to management, because some managers were interested in knowing the amount of LOE being used to support specific tasks. The ISSO decided to identify those charts to the managers who were interested in the information and gain their approval to eliminate them, as it appeared the information provided had met their needs.

The ISSO identified all the metrics charts by objective, the purpose for being developed and used. The charts also would be linked to specific areas that support the TCI and InfoSec plans. The ISSO wanted to be sure that the metrics used to help manage the InfoSec program and the organization met the needs of the InfoSec program.

Metrics charts tend to increase and seem to take on a life of their own. The ISSO was concerned that the time it took to track specific LOEs and projects using metrics was sometimes not cost-effective. By identifying the charts against their purpose in a matrix, the ISSO found that it was easy to analyze the metrics and their purpose (Figure 11.2).

Planning for Next Year

The ISSO received the input from the InfoSec staff at the November meetings and, based on that input, prepared to write next year's InfoSec annual plan and update the InfoSec strategic and tactical plans. However, to accomplish those tasks, the TCI plans had to be received. After all, the InfoSec plans had to support the TCI plans.

The ISSO knew that the draft TCI plans would not be available until January. Therefore, the ISSO drafted the InfoSec annual plan and updated the InfoSec strategic and tactical plans based on the information gathered through discussions with various levels of management involved in developing the TCI Annual Plan and updating the other plans.

Purpose	Chart Identification				
	Chart 1	Chart 2	Chart 3	Chart 4	
Cost	X				
Schedule	X		X	X	
Brief Mgt.		X		X	
Brief Cust.			X		
LOE Drvrs.		X		X	

Figure 11.2 A matrix chart to be used to evaluate metrics charts, based on the charts' purposes.

The ISSO implemented the InfoSec plans January 1, without waiting for the draft TCI plans. The ISSO did so to begin the much-needed LOE modifications and projects that were time dependent. If not started right after the first of the year, their schedules might slip. The ISSO could not afford the slippage and took the risk that the information gathered to date was accurate and any changes at the TCI level would cause only minor adjustments to the InfoSec schedules, if any.

SUMMARY

1. It is a good idea to evaluate the entire InfoSec program on an annual basis.
2. The evaluation should include all projects and LOEs.
3. Changes should be made where value is added in terms of cost decreases, productivity gains, or time savings.
4. Executive management should receive a clear, concise, business-oriented briefing on the state of InfoSec within TCI on an annual basis.
5. Metrics charts should be evaluated annually, and eliminated or modified as necessary.
6. Link analysis methodologies are useful in determining the success of an InfoSec program.

12

21st Century Challenges for the ISSO

CHAPTER OBJECTIVE

The objective of this chapter is to look into the future and discuss the challenges to the ISSO and the risks to information systems and information in the 21st century.

FOUR MAJOR ISSO CHALLENGES FOR THE 21ST CENTURY

In looking at current trends, one can see indications that the ISSO will be challenged to provide InfoSec based on

1. A continued increase and globalization of Internet and its connections to the businesses' and government agencies' intranets (e.g., for electronic commerce),
2. Increasing threats of economic espionage,
3. Increasing potential and threats of the technology-oriented terrorists (techno-terrorists),
4. Concern and potential threats regarding information warfare.

THE INTERNET

The Internet has become an important topic in recent years; and its importance to society, business, and government agencies is expected to increase. Therefore, it will also increase in importance to the 21st century ISSO.

The major technological change making this all possible has been the expansion of networks nationally and internationally. These networks increasingly have gained in importance due to their use and major communication links and international business links.

The backbone of the international network structure has been increasing the access to and use of Internet, which is the major communication and business tool of global commerce. It will continue to expand, as well as the world's use of it.

IMPACT ON CRIME

Crime on the Internet will continue to increase in number and sophistication as more people around the world gain access to it. It is fast becoming an international techno-crime tool. Each system connected to Internet is subject to attack, and many have been attacked. In addition, these attacks are growing in their sophistication and number.

Law enforcement officers are hampered in investigating such attacks by nonexistent laws, lack of jurisdiction, and difficulty in getting cooperation from law enforcement officers of other countries because of politics, different laws, and so forth. For example, what may be illegal in Indonesia may not be illegal in the Netherlands. Therefore, extradition would be impossible, since the citizen of the Netherlands violated no law of his or her country.

The investigation of techno-crimes is complicated enough. When these crimes are accomplished internationally, it is almost impossible to bring the criminals to justice.

WHO ARE THE CULPRITS?

The history of techno-crime cases has shown that these criminals include, but are not limited to,

1.   Internal employees;
2.   Consultants and temporary employees;
3.   Hackers, phreakers, and crackers;
4.   Radicals and terrorists;
5.   Professional techno-criminals for hire.

RISKS DUE TO THE INTERNET

The are many reasons for these risks, such as

1. Global economic competition, where industrial and economic espionage can be conducted with little risk of being caught;
2. The decline of the mainframe systems, increase in LANs and WANs, and the creation of client-server systems—all of which rely more on the users to protect the systems and information than a professional staff of systems personnel;
3. The "Maginot line" mentality of managers and some InfoSec staff members, who look at access control software, firewalls, and passwords as the only security needed;
4. The focus on customer service by network staffs as the highest priority, as well as technical staffs being unfamiliar with their security role;
5. Limited security technology.

The Internet security answer for transmission of information appears to be encryption. Encryption today seems to be in a position similar to the locks of the 1800s. Then, knowledge of locks was not known except by the experts. Criminals needed keys to break in and concentrated on obtaining keys. With the invention of powerful explosives, keys no longer were needed. The criminals just blew off the locks.

The same may be true in the future with encryption, but as we have begun to see, encryption works because the chances of guessing the right key, statistically at least, is almost impossible. However, what if a person guessed it—even guessed it the first time? Also, the more tries at "guessing" the encryption key, the better are your statistical chances of getting it right.

The real problem with encryption is key management, just like we have password management today. Also, with more powerful and cheaper computers, criminals are finding that they can identify encryption keys.

Encryption can protect, with some degree of success, our ability to secure our mail. However, it cannot prevent denial of service, a growing threat.

HOW TO PROTECT THE ORGANIZATION

To protect the corporation or government agency from the Internet problems, the ISSO must have close surveillance of their connections to the Internet itself. Firewall systems must be used to help protect internal networks, routers and internal firewalls to compartmentalize nodes, and security systems for all servers. As InfoSec technology becomes more sophisticated, firewalls probably will be integrated with other pieces of hardware and software, thus providing not only InfoSec but also information throughput and processing. The InfoSec approach is a layered approach, so do not think firewalls are the total answer. Remember IP spoofing, sendmail vulnerabilities?

One-time passwords still may be used but will eventually give way to more bio-medical forms of identification such as retina scans or voice prints.

The Internet will continue expansion to individuals, businesses, and government agencies throughout the world and will do so exponentially. There will be more reliance for contract negotiations and formal contract agreements through the Internet, paving the way for some serious legal issues and contract frauds.

To meet the challenge, the ISSO must understand the Internet and its potential use as a tool as well as the harm it could cause.

THE FUTURE THREATS
OF ECONOMIC ESPIONAGE

When we look at rapid, technology-oriented growth, we find nations of haves and have-nots. We also see corporations that conduct business internationally and those that want to do so. International economic competition and "trade wars" are increasing. Corporations are finding increased competition and looking for that "competitive edge," that competitive advantage.

One way to gain the advantage, the edge, is through industrial and economic espionage. Both forms of espionage have been around since there has been competition. However, in this information age, the competitiveness is more time dependent, more crucial to success, and has increased dramatically, largely due to technology. We see the increased use of technology to steal the competitive advantage and, ironically, these same technology tools are what is being stolen. In addition, we now have more sensitive information consolidated in large databases on internationally networked systems whose security is questionable.

DEFINITIONS OF *INDUSTRIAL* AND
ECONOMIC ESPIONAGE

To clarify what we are talking about here, definitions of *industrial espionage* and *economic espionage* are in order. *Industrial espionage* is defined as an individual or private business entity sponsorship or coordination of intelligence activity conducted to enhance a competitor's advantage in the marketplace. According to the FBI, *economic espionage* is defined as "Government-directed, sponsored, or coordinated intelligence activity, which may or may not constitute violations of law, conducted for the purpose of enhancing that country's or another country's economic competitiveness."

ECONOMICS, WORLD TRADE, AND TECHNOLOGIES

What allowed this proliferation of technologies? Much of it was due to international business relationships among nations and companies. Some of it was due to industrial and economic espionage.

The information age has brought with it more international businesses, more international competitors, and more international businesses working joint projects against international competitors. This has resulted in more opportunities to steal from partners. Also, one may be a business partner on one contract while competing on another, thus providing the opportunity to steal vital economic information. Furthermore, because we now are a world of international business competitors, the world power of a country is determined largely by its economic power. Therefore, in all reality, we are in the midst of worldwide business competition, called by many the economic war.

Even the Russians view economics as a major factor in information warfare. Professor D. S. Chereshkin, vice president of the Russian Academy of Science, Institute of Systems Analysis, Moscow, in a brief thesis entitled, "Realities of Information Warfare," stated:

> . . . The new information technologies, being realized as modern information infrastructure, determine the effectiveness of a country's economy. . . . technologies makes the life fundamentals—power stations and transport system—very sensitive to any destructive influence which can be given to information infrastructure. . . . . . But what types of information weapons are known today?. . . Means for destruction, distortion or plunder of information files. This warfare gives the opportunities to put out of action all highly technological infrastructures . . .

This world competition, coupled with international networks and telecommunication links, has provided more opportunities for more people, such as hackers, phreakers, and crackers, to steal information through these networks. The end of the Cold War also has made many "ex-spies" available to continue to practice their craft but in a capitalistic environment.

ECONOMIC ESPIONAGE VULNERABILITIES

The increase in economic espionage also is due largely to the corporate vulnerability to such threats. Corporations do not adequately identify and protect their information, nor do they adequately protect their computer and telecommunication systems. They lack adequate security policies and procedures; employees are not aware of their responsibility to protect the corporation's proprietary information. Many of the employees and also the managers of these corporations do not believe they have information worth stealing or believe "it can't happen here."

ECONOMIC ESPIONAGE RISKS

When corporations fail to adequately protect their information, they are taking risks that, in all probability, will cause them to lose market share, profits, business, and also help weaken the economic power of their country.

Economic espionage, that espionage supported by a government to further a business, will become more prevalent, more sophisticated, and easier to conduct due to technology.

TECHNO-TERRORISTS' THREATS INTO THE 21ST CENTURY

The 21st century will bring the increased use of technology by terrorists. Today's terrorists not only are using technology to communicate and technology crimes to fund their activities, they are beginning to look at the potential for using technology in the form of information warfare against their enemies. It is estimated that this will increase in the future.

Because today's technology-oriented countries rely on vulnerable computers and telecommunication systems to support their commercial and government operations, it is becoming a concern to businesses and government agencies throughout the world. The advantage to the terrorist of attacking these systems is that the techno-terrorist acts can be done with little expense by very few people and cause a great deal of damage to the economy of a country.

Techno-terrorists can conduct such activities with little risk to themselves, because these systems can be attacked and "destroyed" from the base of a country friendly to them. In addition, they can do so with no loss of life, thus preventing the extreme backlash against them that would occur if they had destroyed buildings with much loss of life.

INFOSEC—MORE IMPORTANT THAN EVER!

The following are some examples of potential techno-terrorists' actions:

1. Terrorists, using a computer, penetrate a control tower computer system and send false signals to aircraft, causing them to crash in midair or into the ground;
2. Terrorists use fraudulent credit cards to finance their operations;
3. Terrorists penetrate a financial computer system and divert millions of dollars to finance their activities;
4. Terrorists bleach U.S. $1 bills and, using a color copier, reproduce them as $100 bills then flood the market with them to destabilize the dollar;
5. Terrorists use cloned cellular phones and computers over the Internet to communicate using encryption to protect their transmissions;

6. Terrorists use virus and worm programs to shut down vital government computer systems;
7. Terrorists change hospital records, causing patients to die from an overdose of medicine or the wrong medicine, or change computerized tests and analysis results;
8. Terrorists penetrate a government computer and cause it to issue checks to all its citizens, thus destabilizing the economy;
9. Terrorists destroy critical government computer systems processing tax returns;
10. Terrorists penetrate computerized train routing systems, causing passenger trains to collide;
11. Terrorists take over telecommunication links or shut them down;
12. Terrorists take over satellite links to broadcast their messages over televisions and radios.

Some may wonder if techno-terrorist activities actually can be considered information warfare (IW). Most IW professionals believe techno-terrorism is part of IW, assuming the attacks are government sponsored and done in support of a foreign government's objectives.

PREVENTION THROUGH AN AGGRESSIVE PROGRAM

To provide for our information system defense, an aggressive program must be implemented. We know our systems are vulnerable to IW attacks. We all know what hackers have done to our systems. Now, imagine what damage can be done by professionally educated and trained IW attack warriors with the full support of a foreign government and millions of dollars to support their efforts; also consider platoons of these IW attack warriors with Ph.D.s in computer science and telecommunications supported by decades of experience in the field, including reverse engineering microprocessors and cloning major computers.

Based on the dependence of a nation's military on the commercial telecommunication infrastructure, as well as on commercial power grids, transportation systems, and the like, the first attack against the United States, or a prelude to that attack, may come in the form of system outages. How does the ISSO professional differentiate between accidents, acts of nature, or human-made attacks?

INFORMATION AGE WARFARE
AND INFORMATION WARFARE

Information warfare is the term being used to define the concept of 21st century warfare, which will be electronic and information systems driven. *Information warfare*, as defined by the U.S. Defense Information Systems Agency

(DISA), involves "actions taken to achieve information superiority in support of national military strategy by affecting adversary information and information systems while leveraging and protecting our information and information systems." This definition seems to be a good summary definition of all the federal government agencies' definitions as noted previously.

The federal government's definition of IW can be divided into three general categories: offensive, defensive, and exploitation. For example,

1. Deny, corrupt, destroy, or exploit an adversary's information, or influence the adversary's perception (Offensive);
2. Safeguard ourselves and allies from similar actions (Defensive) also known as "IW hardening"; and
3. Exploit available information in a timely fashion, in order to enhance our decision/action cycle and disrupt the adversary's cycle (Exploitative).

In addition, the military looks at IW as including electronic warfare (e.g., jamming communications links); surveillance systems, precision strike (e.g., if you bomb a telecommunication switching system, it is IW); and advanced battlefield management (e.g., using information and information systems to provide information on which to base military decisions when at war).

This may be confusing enough, but many, including those in the business sector, believe that information warfare goes far beyond the military-oriented depiction. Others have a broader definition of IW, which includes such things as hackers attacking business systems, governments attacking businesses, even hackers attacking other hackers. These people divide IW into three categories, too, but from a different perspective. They believe that IW should be looked at using the following categories:

1. *Level 1, interpersonal damage,* involves damage to individuals, which would include anything from harassment, privacy loss, to theft of personal information and so forth;
2. *Level 2, intercorporate damage,* involves attacks on businesses and government agencies, which would include such things as theft of computer services or theft of information for industrial espionage;
3. *Level 3, international and inter-trading block damage,* relates to the destabilization of societies and economies, which includes terrorist attacks, economic espionage, and the like.[1]

You will note that this seems to be more of the traditional, business-oriented look at what many call *computer crime* or *high-tech crime.* Using the traditional government view of information warfare, one can make the case for Level 2 and Level 3 coming the closest to the government (primarily, Department of Defense) view of information warfare.

---

[1] See Winn Schwartau's Internet site at http:/www.infowar.com for additional information. This is the premiere site for those interested in all aspects of information warfare.

Still others tend to either separate or combine the terms *information warfare* and *information age warfare*. To differentiate between these two terms is not that difficult. Using the Tofflers' thoughts about the "three waves" as a guide, *information age warfare* easily can be defined as warfare fought in the information age, with information age, computer-based weapons systems, primarily dominated by the use of electronic and information systems.

It is not our intent to establish *the* definition of IW but only to identify it as an issue to be considered when discussing information and information age warfare. After all, because those involved in information warfare cannot agree on the same basic definition, one can see why there is such misunderstanding of its impact on the information security professional.

Those ISSOs within the federal government, and particularly those in the Department of Defense, probably will use the definition related to military actions. ISSOs within the private business sector (assuming they are interested in even using the term *information warfare*) probably would align themselves closer to the definition of those more in the commercial sector. Those ISSOs within the private sector who agree with the government's definition would probably continue to use the computer crime terminology in lieu of the commercial definition.

One may wonder, then, if information warfare is something that the nongovernment, business-oriented ISSO should be concerned about. Each ISSO must be the judge of that based on his or her particular working environment and professional point of view. Regardless, information warfare will grow in importance as a factor to consider, much as viruses, hackers, and other current threats must be considered.

As we enter the 21st century, information warfare, however defined, will have a major impact on how the ISSOs do their jobs. If we refer back to the "business" definition of *information warfare*, we can see that we have been and will continue to be concerned with these types of activities and attacks against the systems for which we are responsible. In all probability, this will have an impact on how we perceive and even how we perform our InfoSec duties in the 21st century.

If we use the government's definition, we, as ISSOs, certainly will be involved. Our involvement will be regardless of whether we are in the government or business sector.

One may wonder how he or she could be involved in a country's information warfare activities—after all, isn't that between governments and their military forces? Nothing can be further from the truth. The Chinese of the People's Republic of China have the view, as do most other countries, that information warfare will include the civilian community:

...The rapid development of networks has turned each automated system into a potential target of invasion. The fact that information technology is increasingly relevant to people's lives determines that those who take part in information war are not all soldiers and that anybody who understands computers may become a "fighter" on the network. Think tanks composed of nongovernmental experts may take part in decision making; rapid mobilization will not just be directed to young people; information-related industries and domains will be the first to be mobilized and enter the war . . . (The British Broadcasting Corporation *Summary of World Broadcasts*, August 20, 1996, translated from the *Jiefangjun Bao* newspaper, Beijing, China, June 25, 1996, p. 6.)

Bill Boni, a highly skilled professional ISSO and friend, said of the ISSO's 21st century challenges:

ISSOs will likely end up in the line of fire in a future type of information warfare (e.g., banking, telecommunications, power grids, transportation). They *will* be the combatants in such conflicts and their systems at risk to the hostilities of the time.

ISSO roles, therefore, will only grow in importance, so new entrants to this fascinating career field will find they have embarked on a lifelong voyage of growth, learning, and discovery. There will be long periods of boring repetition punctuated by moments of adrenaline rush as they face off with a techno-criminal or hostile competitor bent on destruction of the organization's competitive stature. At that moment in time, these ISSOs will learn if their protection mechanisms are up to the challenges of the 21st century.

These people are part of the future "thin blue line," the close alliance of the ISSOs in the organizations and society's protective institutions (law enforcement, national defense) against the rising forces of techno-anarchy and destruction.

Welcome to the front lines!

SUMMARY

1. When a government agency or business computer system is attacked, the response to such an attack will be based on the attacker. Will the attacker be a hacker, phreaker, cracker, or just someone breaking in for fun? Will the attacker be an employee of a business competitor, in the case of an attack on a business system, or will it be a terrorist or government agency-sponsored attacker for economic reasons? Will the attacker be a foreign soldier attacking the system as a prelude to war?

2. The preceding questions require serious consideration when information systems are being attacked, because it dictates the response. Would we attack a country because of what a terrorist or economic spy did to a business or government system?

3. To complicate the matter, what if the terrorist was in a third country but only made it look like he or she was coming from your potential adversary? How do you know?

4. The key to the future is in information systems security for defense and information warfare weapons. As with nuclear weapons used as a form of deterrent, in the future information weapons systems will be the basis of the information warfare deterrent.

5. Each nation must begin now to prepare for 21st century warfare by establishing a program to ensure the protection of information assets in the 21st century.

6. Remember, it is bad enough being attacked, but it is worse to be attacked and not know it until it is too late.

Recommended Reading

Aburdene, Patricia, and John Naisbitt. *Megatrends 2000.* New York: Avon Books, 1990.

Bequai, August. *Techno-Crimes: The Computerization of Crime and Terrorism.* Lexington, MA: D. C. Heath and Co., 1987.

Burger, Ralf. *Computer Viruses: A High-Tech Disease,* 3rd ed. Grand Rapids, MI: Abacus, 1989.

Cheswick, William R., and Steven M. Bellovin. *Firewalls and Internet Security: Repelling the Wily Hacker.* Reading, MA: Addison-Wesley Publishing Co., 1994.

Computer Viruses: Proceedings of an Invitational Symposium, October 10–11, 1988, co-sponsors Deloitte Haskins & Sells and Information Systems Security Association, New York, NY.

DeMaio, Harry B. *Information Protection and Other Unnatural Acts: Every Manager's Guide to Keeping Vital Computer Data Safe and Sound.* New York: Amacom, 1992.

Fernandez, E.B., and others. *The IBM Systems Programming Series: Database Security and Integrity.* Reading, MA: Addison-Wesley Longman 1981.

Fialka, John J., *War by Other Means: Economic Espionage in America.* New York: W. W. Norton & Company, 1997.

Fites, Philip, and Martin P. J. Kratz. *Information Systems Security: A Practitioner's Reference.* New York: Van Nostrand Reinhold, 1993.

Garfinkel, Simson, and Gene Spafford. *Practical UNIX Security.* Sebastopol, CA: O'Reilly & Associates, Inc, 1991.

Hafner, Katie, and John Markoff. *Cyberpunk: Outlaws and Hackers on the Computer Frontier.* New York: Touchstone, 1992.

Ruthberg, Zella G., and Harold F. Tipton, editors. *Handbook of Information Security Management, 1994–95 Yearbook.* Boston: Auerbach Publications, 1994.

Hsiao, David K., and others. *Computer Security.* San Diego, CA: Academic Press, 1979.

Icove, David, and others. *Computer Crime: A Crimefighter's Handbook.* Sebastopol, CA: O'Reilly & Associates, 1995.

Kabay, Michel E. *The NCSA Guide to Enterprise Security: Protecting Information Assets.* New York: McGraw-Hill, 1996.

Kenney, John P., and Harry W. More. *Principles of Investigation,* 2nd ed. St. Paul, MN: West Publishing Co., 1994.

Knightmare, *The Secrets of a Super Hacker.* Port Townsend, WA: Loompanics Unlimited, 1994.

Landreth, Bill, *The Cracker. Out of The Inner Circle: A Hacker's Guide to Computer Security.* Bellevue, WA: Microsoft Press, 1985.

Leibholz, Stephen W., and Louis D. Wilson. *Users' Guide to Computer Crime: Its Commission, Detection and Prevention.* Radnor, PA: Chilton Book Company, 1974.

Mair, William C., and others. *Computer Control and Audit.* 3rd ed. New York: Touche Ross & Co., 1981.

Martin, James. *Security Accuracy and Privacy in Computer Systems.* Englewood Cliffs, NJ: Prentice-Hall, 1973.

McGraw, Gary, and Edward W. Felten. *Java Security: Hostile Applets, Holes, and Antidotes. What Every Netscape and Internet Explorer User Needs to Know.* New York: John Wiley & Sons, 1997.

Naisbitt, John. *Megatrends.* New York: Warner Books, 1982.

Naisbitt, John. *Megatrends Asia.* New York: Simon and Schuster, 1996.

National Research Council. *Computers at Risk: Safe Computing in the Information Age.* Washington, DC: National Academy Press, 1991.

Norman, Adrian R. D. *Computer Insecurity.* New York: Chapman and Hall, 1983.

Ohmae, Kenichi. *The Mind of the Strategist.* Middlesex, England: Penguin Books, 1982.

Parker, Donn B. *Crime by Computer: Startling New Kinds of Million-Dollar Fraud, Theft, Larceny, and Embezzlement.* New York: Charles Scribner & Sons, 1976.

Parker, Donn B. *Computer Security Management.* Reston, VA: Reston Publishing Company, 1981.

Roberts, Ralph. *Computer Viruses.* Greensboro, NC.: Compute! Publications, 1988.

Rose, Lance. *Netlaw: Your Rights in the Online World.* Berkeley. CA: Osborne McGraw-Hill, 1995.

Schwartau, Winn. *Information Warfare: Chaos on the Electronic Superhighway.* New York: Thunder's Mouth Press, 1994.

Schwartau, Winn. *Information Warfare: Cyberterrorism: Protecting Your Personal Security in the Electronic Age,* 2nd ed. New York: Thunder's Mouth Press, 1996.

Schweizer, Peter. *Friendly Spies: How America's Allies Are Using Economic Espionage to Steal Our Secrets.* New York: Atlantic Monthly Press, 1993.

Shaffer, Steven L., and Alan R. Simon. *Network Security.* Cambridge, MA: AP Professional, 1994.

Stang, David J., and Sylvia Moon. *Network Security Secrets.* San Mateo, CA: IDG Books Worldwide, 1993.

Sterling, Bruce. *The Hacker Crackdown: Law and Disorder on the Electronic Frontier.* New York: Bantam Books, 1992.

Toffler, Alvin. *Future Shock.* New York: Bantam Books, 1971.

Toffler, Alvin. *The Third Wave.* New York: Bantam Books, 1980.

Toffler, Alvin. *Powershift.* New York: Bantam Books, 1990.

Toffler, Alvin, and Heidi Toffler. *War and Anti-War.* Boston: Little, Brown and Company, 1993.

Toffler, Alvin, and Heidi Toffler. *Creating a New World Civilization.* Atlanta: Turner Publishing, 1994.

Walker, Bruce J., and Ian F. Blake. *Computer Security and Protection Structures.* Stroudsburg, PA: Dowden, Hutchinson & Ross, Inc., 1977.

Wood, Charles Cresson. *Information Security Policies Made Easy.* Sausalito, CA.: Author, 1994.

About the Author

Dr. Gerald L. Kovacich, CFE, CPP, CISSP, graduated from the University of Maryland with a bachelor's degree in history and politics, with emphasis in Asia; the University of Northern Colorado with a master's degree in social science with emphasis in public administration; Golden Gate University with a master's degree in telecommunications management; the U.S. Department of Defense Language Institute (Chinese Mandarin); and August Vollmer University with a doctorate in criminology. He also is a Certified Fraud Examiner, Certified Protection Professional, and a Certified Information Systems Security Professional.

Dr. Kovacich has over 36 years of industrial security, investigations, information systems security, and information warfare experience in both government and business. He has worked for numerous technology-based international corporations as an ISSO, security, audit, and investigations manager and consultant. He developed and managed several internationally based InfoSec programs for Fortune 500 corporations and managed several information systems security organizations, including providing service and support for their information warfare products and services.

He has taught both graduate and undergraduate courses in criminal justice, technology crime investigations, and security for Los Angeles City College, DeAnza College, Golden Gate University, and August Vollmer University. He also lectured internationally and presented workshops on these topics for national and international conferences and has had numerous articles published on high-tech crime investigations, information systems security, and information warfare, both nationally and internationally.

Currently, Dr. Kovacich is the President of Information Security Management Associates, a Mission Viejo, California-based information systems protection and high-tech crime investigations consulting firm; Associate, PT Citamulia Prajakonsulindo, an Indonesian-based banking and business consulting firm, and Associate, Safetynet Services consultant, a Malaysian-based security consulting firm. Dr. Kovacich chairs the Association of Certified Fraud Examiner's Computer Fraud Committee and is its representative for South East Asian nations.

Index

Other Books from Butterworth-Heinemann

Art of Successful Security Management
Dennis R. Dalton
1997   312pp   hc   0-7506-9729-6

Computer Security, Third Edition
John M. Carroll
1995   560pp   hc   0-7506-9600-1

Managing Legal and Security Risks in Computing and Communications
Paul Shaw
1997   224pp   pb   0-7506-9938-8

Protecting Business Information: A Manager's Guide
James A. Schweitzer
1995   234pp   hc   0-7506-9658-3

Ultimate Computer Security Survey
James L. Schaub and Ken D. Biery, Jr.
1995   200pp with 3.5" ASCII disk   pb   0-7506-9692-3

Detailed information on these and all other BH-Security titles may be found in the BH-Security catalog(Item #800). To request a copy, call 1-800-366-2665. You can also visit our web site at: http://www.bh.com

These books are available from all good bookstores or in case of difficulty call: 1-800-366-2665 in the U.S. or +44-1865-310366 in Europe.

E-Mail Mailing List

An e-mail mailing list giving information on latest releases, special promotions/ offers and other news relating to BH-Security titles is available. To subscribe, send an e-mail message to majordomo@world.std.com. Include in message body (not in subject line) subscribe bh-security